KNITTING HATS &
MITTENS FROM AROUND
THE WORLD

34 HEIRLOOM PATTERNS
IN A VARIETY OF STYLES
AND TECHNIQUES

Kari Cornell, Editor

Voyageur Press

CONTENTS

INTRODUCTION

BY DONNA DRUCHUNAS

Almost four thousand years ago, an artist stood inside a tomb in Thebes. In the dark enclosure, illuminated only by the flickering flame of a torch or oil lamp, he painted a stick figure of a man wearing a cone-shaped straw hat. This early depiction of a hat suggests that head coverings were perhaps first worn in the Far East, possibly China.

Ancient Persians, Greeks, and Romans all wore some type of head covering. In Persia, many styles of hats were popular, including an egg-shaped felt hat, which may have been one of the earliest hats worn to protect against cold. The Phrygian cap, a fitted cone-shaped red cap, was worn throughout Persia and Central Asia. Greek sailors and travelers wore a similar brimless cap, made of leather or felt, called a *pileus*. Later worn by freed slaves in Rome, this style never went completely out of fashion and became the precursor to today's knitted ski caps.

THE FIRST GLOVES

In one version of Homer's *Odyssey*, Laërtes pulled down his sleeves to cover his hands while walking through a garden riddled with brambles. In other translations, he is wearing gloves to protect his skin from scratches. Before separate hand coverings came into use, people often pulled long sleeves down over their hands when performing certain tasks, and the earliest gloves were simple bags with no finger or thumb openings.

KNITTED HATS AND GLOVES IN EUROPE

During the Middle Ages, a number of felted wool hat styles came into popularity. The earliest were made from fleece felted over a hat form, and some may have been examples of *nålbinding*, a northern European needlework technique in which fabric that looks knitted or crocheted is created using a large sewing needle.

Toques, popular around Europe as early as the twelfth and thirteenth centuries, were close-fitting wool hats that resembled Roman-style Phrygian caps. By the late sixteenth century, black velvet toques were in vogue among both men and women, and women wore them into the nineteenth century.

Hats were probably the first items to be knitted in England. The village of Monmouth became famous for its close-fitting knitted and felted caps in the fifteenth and sixteenth centuries. In Scotland, this fashion lasted well into the eighteenth century.

People began to knit mittens and gloves in the Middle Ages as well. Ladies began wearing gloves in the thirteenth century, but the fashion exploded when Queen Elizabeth I commissioned a pair of elaborately embroidered and bejeweled gloves, specifically so she could remove them in public and draw attention to her beautiful hands. Glove making, a serious business in the sixteenth century, was governed by strict guild rules. Only after five years of apprenticeship could a professional knitter attempt a pair of gloves, and imperfect samples would be burned.

Although stranded colorwork knitting had been used for centuries in the south of Europe, mittens made with multiple strands of wool yarn became popular in northern Europe only during the eighteenth and nineteenth centuries. Knitters in Scandinavia and the Baltics (Estonia, Latvia, and Lithuania) were knitting more elaborately patterned mittens and gloves, sometimes using traditional weaving or embroidery patterns.

HATS AND GLOVES IN THE NEW WORLD

With the migration of knitting to the Americas, designs from many different parts of Europe evolved into recognizable new styles, unique to different regions in the Western Hemisphere. In Canada, the toque, a distant relative of the Phrygian cap, has become a national emblem. The red toque, first recognized as a symbol of liberty in Rome, was revived by the French in 1837 when they battled the British for control over what would become the Canadian province of Quebec. The French wore the red toques as a symbol of patriotism.

The Spanish brought knitting to the Andes, and the people of South America quickly adapted the patterns from their existing textile traditions to motifs in knitting. Men and boys knit and wear tight-fitted, multicolored caps with ear flaps, known as *ch'ullus*. Boys learn to knit at a young age and make all of their own caps.

A man knits a *ch'ullu*, the traditional hat worn in the Andes Mountains of South America. *Photo by Cynthia LeCount Samaké—Behind the Scenes Adventures: www.btsadventures.com*

Many of the projects on the pages of this book draw inspiration from popular hat and mitten styles throughout history. Whether you're looking for an easy project or something more challenging, you'll find patterns in this collection that you'll love to knit and wear. So break out your needles, and get ready to cast on! ❧

HATS AND MITTENS OF SCANDINAVIA

FINNISH PÄIVÄTÄR HAT AND MITTENS

DESIGN BY HEATHER ORDOVER

This set is named after Päivätär, the Sun Goddess in the Finnish epic poem *The Kalevala*. Not only was Päivätär a goddess, she was a goddess of spinning, and her sister, goddess of the moon, was in charge of weaving. In this pattern you'll see the sun rise up the back of the mittens and ripples of color, like plies, cross the palms. The trellis pattern in the hatband and mitten gauntlet was used in both knitting and weaving. This design is based on traditional Finnish hats—the type you might see as part of a national costume—which were generally woven garments that were pieced and sewn together with longer than usual earflaps. ✌

HAT

Size
Woman's Medium-Large

Finished Measurements
Circumference at head: Approx 22"/56cm
Length (bottom of earflap to foldline): Approx 10"/25.5cm

Materials
- Brown Sheep Lanaloft worsted, 100% wool, 100g/3.5oz, 160yds/146m, LL15S Roasted Pepper #006, 1 skein
- Brown Sheep Lamb's Pride worsted, 85% wool/15% mohair, 113g/4oz, 190yds/174m, M140 Aran #095, 1 skein
- Two size 8 (5mm) 24"/61.5cm or 36"/91.5cm long circular needles or size needed to obtain gauge
- Size 000 (1.25mm) double-pointed needle (optional for I-cord)
- Stitch markers
- Split-ring stitch markers
- Tapestry needle

Gauge
20 sts and 20 rows = 4"/10cm in St st.
Adjust needle size as necessary to obtain correct gauge.

MITTENS

Size
Woman's Average

Finished Measurements
Circumference around hand: 7½"/19cm
Length: 10"/25.5cm
Note: To fit a 7"/18cm palm circumference and a 7¾"/19.5cm long woman's hand (measuring from base of palm to tip of longest finger).

Materials
- The March Hare worsted, 100% wool, 100g/3.5oz, 440yds/402m, Cream (MC), 1 skein
- The March Hare silk blend, 70% merino/30% silk, 100g/3.5oz, 435yds/398m, Scarlet Letter (CC), 1 skein
- Size 0 (2mm) 24"/61cm and 36"/91.5cm circular needles or size needed to obtain gauge
- Stitch markers
- Tapestry needle

Gauge
34 sts and 37 rows = 4"/10cm in St st.
Adjust needle size as necessary to obtain correct gauge.

PATTERN NOTES

Construction: In order to have a continuous plaited border to the hat, "extra" stitches had to be counted in to create the vertical edges of the earflaps. From the beginning of the round, the first earflap will require 40 stitches, the back of the hat will use 30, the second earflap will use 40 stitches, and the front of the hat will use the remaining 50 stitches. This is also why knitting on two circular needles is useful for this hat—the number of stitches is quite large at the outset but decreases markedly once the earflaps are complete. The earflaps have a "center line" of paired decreases and matching edge decreases that "seam" the earflap to the plaited border. This construction, when complete, will leave a total of 14 stitches remaining at the top of the earflap, which is now the lower edge of the hatband proper.

HAT INSTRUCTIONS

To CO, loosely knot MC and CC1 around one circular needle. *Do not count this st in your CO.*

Hold the CC over your index finger and the MC over your thumb. This will give you two separate rows of color for your CO edge.

Using the long-tail method and the two colors, CO 160 sts. Using two circular needles, distribute sts evenly and join carefully in the round, making sure not to twist sts.

Plaited Edge

Note: The plaited edge will roll. Depending on your process, let that roll determine your "right" and "wrong" side (or red or white dominant side). The sample you see here has a dominant red side as the "right" side, and thus a red bonnet in back.

Rnd 1: With yarns in back, k1 MC, k1 CC around (end with CC).

Rnd 2: Bring yarns to front, p1 MC, p1 CC around, keeping yarn in front and bringing working yarn over the top of the previous color.

Rnd 3: Keep yarns in front, p1 MC, p1 CC, bringing working yarn under previous color.

Optional Rep: Rnds 1–3 once.

Rnd 4: Bring yarns to back, then [k1 MC, k1 CC] around.

Earflap

At start of rnd, pm, count 40 sts and place the split-ring marker. This is where the first earflap will end when the decs are complete. Skip next 30 sts for the back, pm, count 40 sts and place another split-ring marker. This is where the second earflap will end when the decs are complete. The rem 50 sts are the front sts.

First Earflap

Row 1 (RS): K24.

Row 2 (WS): Sl 1 wyif, p5.

Row 3: Sl 1, ssk, k2tog, k2, ssk.

Row 4: Sl 1 wyif, p6, p2tog.

Row 5: Sl 1, k7, ssk.

Row 6: Sl 1 wyif, p8, p2tog.

Row 7: Sl 1, k2, ssk, k2tog, k3, ssk.

Row 8: Sl 1 wyif, p8, p2tog.

Row 9: Sl 1, k2, ssk, k2tog, k3, ssk.

Row 10: Sl 1 wyif, p8, p2tog.

Row 11: Sl 1, k2, ssk, k2tog, k4.

Row 12: Sl 1 wyif, p9.

Row 13: Sl 1, k10.

Row 14: Sl 1 wyif, p11.

Row 15: Sl 1, k3, ssk, k2tog, k4, ssk.

Row 16: Sl 1 wyif, p10, p2tog.

Row 17: Sl 1, k11, ssk.

Row 18: Sl 1 wyif, p12, k2tog.

Row 19: Sl 1, k4, ssk, k2tog, k5, ssk.

Row 20: Sl 1 wyif, p9, k1, p2, k2tog.

Place 14 sts on a holder.

Second Earflap

Work same as First Earflap.

Body

There should be 108 sts on the rnd—14 sts earflap, 50 sts front, 14 sts earflap, 30 sts back. Knit Rnds 1–24 foll 36-st rep Hat Chart A, pm after each 36 sts and rep sts 1–36 three times to create the entire, continuous front band.

Crown

Set-up Rnd: Using MC only, purl around, pm every 12 sts (9 sections total).

Rnd 1: *Knit to 2 sts before marker, k2tog; rep from * around.

Rnd 2: Knit.

Rnds 3–6: *Knit to 2 sts before marker, k2tog; rep from * around.

Rnd 7: Knit.

Rnds 8–12: *Knit to 2 sts before marker, k2tog rep from * around.

Rnd 13: Knit.

Rnd 14: *Knit to 2 sts before marker, k2tog; rep from * around.

Rnd 15: K2tog around—9 sts.

Break yarn, leaving an 8"/20.5cm tail.
With tapestry needle, thread tail through rem 9 sts and pull tight. Secure tail on WS.

Finishing

Weave in all ends and block as necessary.

PATTERN NOTES

If you are at all concerned about making two left-thumbed mittens rather than a pair with the thumbs in the correct place, you may wish to knit two at a time on the circular needles. This pattern lends itself well to either double-pointed needles or circular needles.

A larger size can be achieved by going up a needle size or two. Use your hand measurements and a gauge swatch to check. If that option won't work for you, either add or subtract the edge stitches that run up the outer edge of the mitten itself. For a more flared gauntlet, add one or more of the geometric bands of 2x2 color squares that run up the outer edge of the back of the mittens (column 174–181). These could be placed between two pattern reps throughout the gauntlets, indicating the outside edge of the hand. Those stitches could then become the same columns (column 174–181) in the hand pattern.

MITTENS INSTRUCTIONS

Loosely knot MC and CC1 around one circular needle. *Do not count this st in your CO.* Hold the CC over your index finger and the MC over your thumb. This will give you two separate rows of color for your CO edge. Using the long-tail method and the two colors, CO 80 sts. PM for beg of rnd and join, taking care not to twist sts.

Plaited Edge

Note: The plaited edge will roll. Depending on your process, let that roll determine your "right" and "wrong" side (or red or white dominant side). The sample you see here has a dominant red side as the "right" side, and thus a red bonnet in back.

Rnd 1: With yarns in back, k1 MC, k1 CC around (end with CC).

Rnd 2: Bring yarns to front, p1 MC, p1 CC around, keeping yarn in front and bringing working yarn over the top of the previous color.

Rnd 3: Keep yarns in front, p1 MC, p1 CC, bringing working yarn under previous color.

Optional Rep: Knit Rnds 1–3 once.

Rnd 4: Bring yarns to back, then [k1 MC, k1 CC] around. **Optional:** for a very neat edge, use this rnd to pick up the CO sts one at a time to knit tog with the sts on the needle to create a more solid "tube" of plaiting.

Gauntlet, Hand, and Thumb

Follow Gauntlet Chart B. (**Note:** Row 35 is the dec rnd.) Knit in pat, using black boxes indicated as the insert site for thumb gussets. Foll Hand/Thumb Chart C, inserting right and left thumb gussets as appropriate. Cont gusset incs to row indicated by the top of each black box. Place thumb sts onto a holder or waste yarn when knitting first complete rnd after black boxes are complete. CO 4 sts to replace thumb gusset sts.

Knit to Row 58 to begin hand decs. Dec as indicated on chart, every row, paired decs leaning into middle of mitten. When 8 sts are left (4 border sts and 4 center sts) on each side, BO with Kitchener stitch as you would with a sock toe. Alternately, use a three-needle BO with the mitten pulled inside out.

Place thumb sts on needle, pick up 12 sts to form the "inside" of the thumb. **Note:** Two different pattern choices are shown. The sample was knitted with the pattern that continues the edge pattern, making a virtually invisible thumb when mitten is flat.

Once sts are picked up, begin thumb with Rnd 22 and foll the appropriate thumb chart. Use Kitchener stitch to close.

Finishing

Weave in all ends.
Turn mitten right side out, block lightly.

FINNISH PÄIVÄTÄR HAT CHART

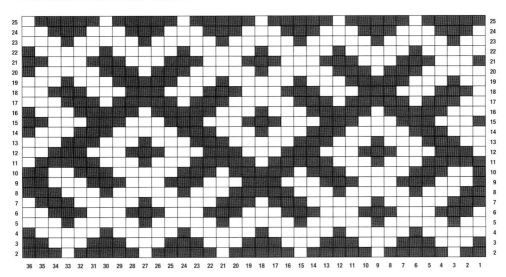

KEY
■ Color 1
□ Color 2

FINNISH PÄIVÄTÄR HAT EARFLAP CHART

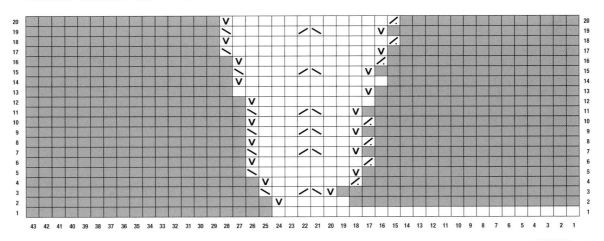

KEY
� SSK
◸ K2tog
◿ p2tog
V Slip
▨ No Stitch

FINNISH PÄIVÄTÄR MITTEN GAUNTLETS CHART

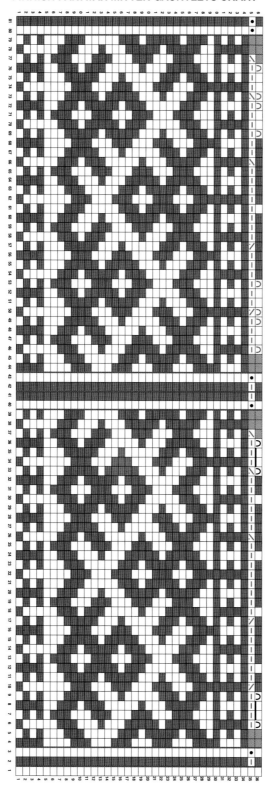

FINNISH PÄIVÄTÄR MITTEN CHART

KEY

■	Color 1
□	Color 2
⊟	Purl Color 1
•	Purl Color 2
◩	P2tog tbl
◪	P2tog
▨	No Stitch
⋒	Twisted Purl Color 1
⋒	Twisted Purl Color 2

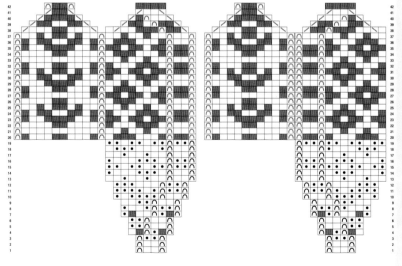

THUMB CHART

15

SUNNHORDALAND HAT AND MITTENS

DESIGN BY BETH BROWN-REINSEL

I love to design with motifs from long ago, knit in a high gauge for lots of detail. This mitten and hat set was inspired by a sweater knitted in the nineteenth century, from Sunnhordaland, Norway. I first saw this sweater in the book *Nordic Knitting* by Susanne Pagoldh (Interweave Press, 1991). I added a facing for the cuffs and the brim of the hat to increase warmth and longevity. This is created with a provisional cast on and a picot turning edge for a crisp beginning to all the pieces. ❧

HAT

Sizes
Children's Large/Adult's Small (Adult's Medium/Large)

Finished Measurements
Circumference at head: Approx 21 (23)"/53.5 (58.5)cm
Length: Approx 8¼ (9¼)"/21 (23.5)cm

Materials
- Red Fish Dyeworks 20/2 50% silk, 50% Merino wool, 50g/1.75oz, 400yds/366m, Blue #BP613a (MC), Yellow: #Y4e (CC1), Green: #Y-YGBL4a (CC2) and Maria's Red (CC3), 1 skein each
- Size 000 (1.25 mm) 16"/ 40.5cm circular needle long or size needed to obtain gauge
- Size 000 (1.25mm) double-pointed needles (www.lacis.com)
- Stitch marker
- Waste yarn
- Tapestry needle

Gauge
54 sts and 55 rows = 4"/10cm in St st.
Adjust needle size as necessary to obtain correct gauge.

MITTENS

Sizes
Child's Large (Adult's Small/Medium, Adult's Large)

Finished Measurements
Circumference around palm: 7 (8, 9)"/ 18 (20, 22.75)cm
Length: 8 (10¾, 12)"/20.5 (27.5, 30.5)cm

Materials
- Red Fish Dyeworks 20/2 50% silk, 50% Merino wool, 50g/1.75oz, 400yds/366m, Blue: #BP613a (MC), Yellow: #Y4e (CC1), Green: #Y-YGBL4a (CC2) and Maria's Red CC3), 1 skein each (or remaining Maria's Red and Green from the hat) (www.redfishdyeworks.com)
- Size 000 (1.25 mm) double-pointed needles (www.lacis.com)
- Stitch marker
- Waste yarn
- Tapestry needle

Gauge
54 sts and 55 rows = 4"/10 cm in St st.
Adjust needle size as necessary to obtain correct gauge.

SPECIAL TECHNIQUE

Invisible Cast-on: Make a slipknot with two yarns (your working yarn and a contrast yarn) leaving 4"/10cm tails. Hold the two yarns with your left hand at right angles to each other with the contrast yarn in front, while holding the tails out of the way with your right hand, which is also holding the needle. *Take your needle over and behind the working yarn, over and in front of the contrast yarn, over and behind the working yarn again, then under and in front of the contrast yarn—two stitches cast on. Repeat from * until you have the desired number of stitches. Turn work without letting go of the yarns and knit the stitches with your working yarn.

SPECIAL ABBREVIATIONS

CDD (Center Double Decrease): Slip 2 tog k-wise, k1, p2sso.

HAT INSTRUCTIONS

Hat Facing

With CC1, waste yarn and circular needle, invisibly CO 242 (276) sts. Pm for beg of rnd and join, taking care not to twist sts. Work in St st for 2.5"/6.5cm. Inc 28 (30) sts evenly in next rnd—270 (306) sts. Work 2 more rnds in CC1.

Picot Edge

Rnd 1: *K2tog, yo; rep from * around.

Knit 1 rnd.

Brim

Join MC and knit 3 rnds.

Work 18-st rep of Chart A 15 (17) times across the rnd, adding CC2 and CC3 when needed. When complete, weave in all ends.

Remove the waste yarn from the invisible CO, placing the sts on dpns. Be certain that all the sts of the invisible CO are sitting on the needles all the same way. (The invisible CO creates sts where every other one sits twisted on the needle.) Fold work so that the needles are parallel and the patterned area is on the outside and the facing is inside.

Using circular needle and MC, *put the right needle into the first st on the first needle, then into the first st on the second needle (dpn). Knit the sts tog as one st (one new st on right needle). Rep from * across rnd, skipping an inside facing st approx every 9th st—270 (306) sts.

Crown

Knit 1 rnd in MC, inc 10 (2) sts—280 (308) sts. Work 14-st rep of Chart B 20 (22) times across rnd, working Rnds 1–26 twice for a total of 52 rnds. Break off CC1 and CC2.

Decreases

Rnd 1: Cont with MC yarn only and dec 0 (4) sts evenly around—280 (304) sts.

Rnd 2: *K32 (35), CDD; rep from * around—264 (288) sts.

Rnd 3 and all odd rnds: Knit even.

Rnd 4: *K30 (33), CDD; rep from * around—248 (272) sts.

Rnd 6: *K28 (31), CDD; rep from * around—232 (256) sts.

Rnd 8: *K26 (29), CDD; rep from * around—216 (240) sts.

Rnd 10: *K24 (27), CDD; rep from * around—200 (224) sts.

Rnd 12: *K22 (25), CDD; rep from * around—184 (208) sts.

Rnd 14: *K20 (23), CDD; rep from * around—168 (192) sts.

Rnd 16: *K18 (21), CDD; rep from * around—152 (176) sts.

Rnd 18: *K16 (19), CDD; rep from * around—136 (160) sts.

Rnd 20: *K14 (17), CDD; rep from * around—120 (144) sts.

Rnd 22: *K12 (15), CDD; rep from * around—104 (128) sts.

Rnd 24: *K10 (13), CDD; rep from * around—88 (112) sts.

Rnd 26: *K8 (11), CDD; rep from * around—72 (96) sts.

Rnd 28: *K6 (9), CDD; rep from * around—56 (80) sts.

Rnd 30: *K4 (7), CDD; rep from * around—40 (64) sts.

Rnd 32: *K2 (5), CDD; rep from * around—24 (48) sts.

Child's Large/Adult's Small Size Only

Rnd 34: *K2tog; rep from * around—12 sts.

Rnd 36: *K2tog; rep from * around—6 sts.

Break yarn and draw through rem sts. Fasten off.

Adult's Medium/Large Size Only

Rnd 34: *K(3), CDD; rep from * around—32 sts,

Rnd 36: *K(1), CDD; rep from * around—16 sts.

Rnd 38: *K2tog; rep from * around—8 sts.

Break yarn, leaving a 6"/15cm tail. With tapestry needle, thread tail through rem sts, pull tight. Secure to WS.

Finishing

Weave in all ends. Fold facing to WS along picot edge and sew in place. Wash, rinse, and roll in towel to blot excess water. Lay flat to dry.

If desired, make a tassel and sew to top of hat.

MITTENS INSTRUCTIONS

Mitten Facing

Using CC1, waste yarn, and dpn, invisibly CO 65 (81, 98) sts; divide sts on three dpns. Pm for beg of rnd and join, being careful not to twist sts.

Child's Large Size Only

Work in St st for 2"/5cm, inc 7 sts evenly in the next rnd—72 sts.

Cont in CC1 until piece measures approx 2.25"/5.75cm.

Adult's Small/Medium and Adult's Large Sizes Only

Work in St st for 2.5"/6.5cm, inc (9, 10) sts evenly in next rnd—(90, 108) sts.

Cont in CC1 until piece meas approx 3"/7.5cm.

All sizes

Picot edge

Rnd1: *K2tog, yo; rep from * around.

Knit 1 rnd.

Join MC and knit 3 rnds.

Work Chart A 18-st rep 4 (5, 6) times across the rnd, adding CC2 and CC3 when needed. When complete, weave in all ends, except those still attached to the balls of yarn.

Remove waste yarn from invisible CO, placing sts on dpns. Be certain that all the sts of the invisible CO are sitting on the needles all the same way. (The invisible CO creates sts where every other one sits twisted on the needle.) Fold work so that the needles are parallel and the patterned area is on the outside and the facing is inside.

Using a dpn and MC, *put right needle into the first st on the first needle, then into the first st on the second needle. Knit the sts tog as one st (one new st on right needle). Rep from * across row, skipping an inside facing st approx every tenth st—72 (90, 108) sts.

Knit 1 rnd in MC, inc 26 (22, 18) sts evenly spaced—98 (112, 126) sts.

Work 14-st rep of Chart B 7 (8, 9) times across rnd, working 13 (39, 39) rnds of chart.

Thumb Gussets

Note: *A piece of waste yarn is inserted into the body of the mitten where the thumb will eventually be.*

Right Hand

Work in pat over 56 (63, 70) sts. Drop the working yarns. With waste yarn, knit next 16 (20, 22) sts for thumb gusset. Slide these sts back to the left needle and work them and the rem sts of the rnd in the est pat.

Left Hand

Work in pat over 26 (29, 34) sts. Drop the working yarns. With waste yarn, knit the next 16 (20, 22) sts for thumb gusset. Slide these sts back to the left needle and work them and the rem sts of the rnd in est pat.

Main Mitten

Cont in est pat until length from picot edge is 6½ (9¼, 10)"/16.5 (23.5, 25.5) cm or until 1¼ (1¾, 2)"/3 (4.25, 5) cm less than desired length. **Note:** There should be approx 4 (6½, 7) star motifs in the length of the mitten body.

Top Decreases

Rnd 1: *Ssk, work across 45 (52, 59) sts, k2tog, pm, rep from * around.

Rnd 2: *Ssk, work to 2 sts before midpoint marker, k2tog; rep from * around.

Cont dec every rnd as in Rnd 2 until 26 (28, 30) sts rem. **Note:** If a star has been completed and you still need more length, work in MC to end, rather than knitting a partial motif. Using Kitchener stitch, join rem sts tog.

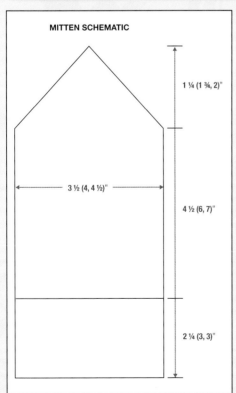

MITTEN SCHEMATIC

1 ¼ (1 ¾, 2)"

3 ½ (4, 4 ½)"

4 ½ (6, 7)"

2 ¼ (3, 3)"

Thumb

Remove waste yarn. With dpns, pick up the resulting loops. There should be 16 (20, 22) sts below the hole and 16 (20, 22) sts above the hole. Join MC at the side of the thumb, pm for beg of rnd, and pick up a st at each side of the thumb—34 (42, 46) sts.

Rnd 1: *K2tog, k13 (17, 19) sts, ssk; rep from * around—30 (38, 42) sts.

Rnd 2: Knit even.

Rnd 3: *K2tog, k11 (15, 17) sts, ssk; rep from * around—26 (34, 38) sts.

Cont even until thumb is approx 5"/12.5cm or desired length.

Decreases

Rnd 1: *Ssk, k9 (13, 15) sts, k2tog: pm, rep from * around—22 (30, 34) sts.

Rnd 2: *Ssk, k to 2 sts before second marker, k2tog; rep from * around—18 (26, 30) sts.

Rep Rnd 2 until 10 sts rem.

Using Kitchener stitch, join rem sts tog.

Finishing

Weave in all ends. Fold facing to WS along picot edge and sew in place. Wash, rinse, and roll in towel to blot excess water. Lay flat to dry.

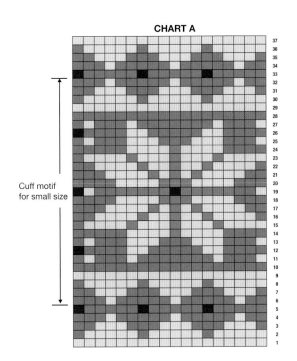

CHART A

Cuff motif for small size

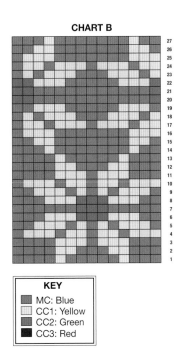

CHART B

KEY	
	MC: Blue
	CC1: Yellow
	CC2: Green
	CC3: Red

WINTER GARDEN HAT AND MITTENS

DESIGN BY DAWN BROCCO

By inserting purl stitches into what would normally be a Fair Isle motif, this stunning set becomes a Bohus-inspired design. The purl stitches and a third color add texture and highlighting to the hat and mittens and make the motif sing. The angora blend Cascade Yarns Cloud 9 adds to the beauty of this Bohus-inspired design and mimicks the angora blend yarn added to the original Bohus-inspired designs. Garter ridges on the hat and mitten cuffs naturally form a turning row for the stockinette lining. I used a deep lining on the hat to add warmth around the ears, but a short lining on the mitten cuffs, where extra warmth isn't needed. ❧

HAT

Size
Woman's Average

Finished Measurements
Circumference at head: Approx 20½"/52cm
Length (not including loops): Approx 8"/20.5cm

Materials
- ◆ Cascade Yarns Cloud 9, 50% angora/50% wool, 100g/3.5oz, 220yds/201m, Natural #101 (MC) Navy #119 (CC1), 1 skein each
- ◆ Cascade 220 wool, 100% Peruvian wool, 50g/1.75oz, 164yds/150m, Bluebell #7816 (CC2), 1 skein
- ◆ Size 7 (4.5mm)16"/40.5cm circular needle or size needed to obtain gauge
- ◆ Size 7 (4.5mm) double-pointed needles
- ◆ Sizes G/6 (4mm) or H/8 (5mm) crochet hook
- ◆ Stitch holder
- ◆ Stitch marker
- ◆ Tapestry needle

Gauge
24 sts and 30 rows = 4"/10 cm in St st.
21 sts and 24 rows = 4"/10m in charted pattern.
Adjust needle size as necessary to obtain correct gauge.

MITTENS

Size
Woman's Average

Finished Measurements
Circumference around hand: 7½"/19cm
Length: 7¾"/19.5cm

Materials
- ◆ Cascade Yarns Cloud 9, 50% angora/50% wool, 100g/3.5oz, 220yds/201m, Natural #101 (MC), Navy #119 (CC1), 1 skein each
- ◆ Cascade 220 wool, 100% Peruvian wool, 50g/1.75oz, 164yds/150m, Bluebell #7816 (CC2), 1 skein
- ◆ Sizes 6 (4mm), 7 (4.5mm), and 8 (5mm) double-pointed needles or size needed to obtain gauge
- ◆ Sizes G/6 (4mm) or H/8 (5mm) crochet hook
- ◆ Smooth waste yarn for provisional CO
- ◆ Stitch holder
- ◆ Stitch marker
- ◆ Tapestry needle

Gauge
24 sts and 30 rows = 4"/10cm in St st with size 6 (4mm) needles.
21 sts and 24 rows = 4"/10cm in charted pattern with size 7 (4.5mm) needles.

SPECIAL ABBREVIATIONS

M1: Place twisted loop onto right-hand needle.

PATTERN NOTES

Using three colors, and purling, can seem unwieldy and tedious. Break short lengths 2–4"/5–10cm of CC1 and CC2, so you can pull them out of the yarn fray that will ensue.

HAT INSTRUCTIONS

With MC and dpns, using long-tail CO method, CO 6 sts; divide evenly onto three dpns. Pm for beg of rnd and join, taking care not to twist sts.

Rnd 1: (K1, M1) 6 times—12 sts.

Rnd 2: (K2, M1) 6 times—18 sts.

Rnd 3: (K3, M1) 6 times—24 sts.

Rnd 4: (K4, M1) 6 times—30 sts.

Rnd 5: (K5, M1) 6 times—36 sts.

Rnd 6: (K6, M1) 6 times—42 sts.

Rnd 7: (K7, M1) 6 times—48 sts.

Rnd 8: (K8, M1) 6 times—54 sts.

Rnd 9: (K9, M1) 6 times—60 sts.

Rnd 10 and even-numbered rnds: Knit.

Rnd 11: (K10, M1) 6 times—66 sts.

Rnd 13: (K11, M1) 6 times—72 sts.

Rnd 15: (K12, M1) 6 times—78 sts.

Rnd 17: (K13, M1) 6 times—84 sts.

Rnd 19: (K14, M1) 6 times—90 sts.

Rnd 21: (K15, M1) 6 times—96 sts.

Rnd 23: (K16, M1) 6 times—102 sts.

Rnd 25: (K17, M1) 6 times—108 sts.

Rnd 26: Knit. Don't break MC.

With CC2 knit, inc 2 sts evenly on next rnd—110 sts.

Change to circular needle and pm at beg of rnd.

Purl 1 rnd. Do not break CC2.

With CC1, knit 1 rnd. Purl 1 rnd. Do not break CC1.

With MC, knit 1 rnd. Purl 1 rnd. Knit 1 rnd.

Foll 10-st rep of Winter Garden Chart for 21 rnds. Do not break CC1 and CC2.

With MC, knit 2 rnds. Purl 1 rnd.

With CC1, knit 1 rnd. Purl 1 rnd. Break CC1.

With CC2, knit 1 rnd. Purl 1 rnd. Break CC2.

Facing

With MC, knit 34 rnds (approx 5½"/14cm). BO.

Finishing

With tapestry needle, sew down facing inside hat, approx on the 2nd MC rnd, past the CC1 garter ridge. The CC2 turning ridge should lie flat around the hat's lower edge.

Top Chain Loops

Break a 2"/5cm long length of CC1 and CC2.

With crochet hook, leave a small tail and chain 18 with CC1.

Pull rem yarn end through last loop to end off. Rep with CC2.

Place both chains side by side.

Thread one group of yarn ends into tapestry needle and insert at top of hat to WS.

Thread other group of tails and insert into top of hat 1 st over from last insertion.

On inside of hat, double overhand knot both groups of ends, then double overhand knit them again. Pull snug and trim excess. Weave in all ends.

MITTEN INSTRUCTIONS

Note: The mittens are worked in two directions. The hand is worked from the crochet provisional CO down. Then the cuff is worked by picking up sts from the CO sts.

With smooth waste yarn, chain 46 sts, to allow enough room for picking up error.

With MC and size 6 dpns, pick up and k1 st into the back loops of the center 40 sts on the chain. Knit 1 rnd.

Thumb Gusset

Right Hand

Rnd 1: K3, M1, k1, M1, knit to end of rnd—42 sts.

Rnds 2–3: Knit.

Rnd 4: K3, M1, k3, M1, knit to end of rnd—44 sts.

Rnds 5–6: Knit.

Rnd 7: K3, M1, k5, M1, knit to end of rnd—46 sts.

Rnds 8–9: Knit.

Rnd 10: K3, M1, k7, M1, knit to end of rnd—48 sts.

Rnds 11–12: Knit.

Rnd 13: K3, M1, k9, M1, knit to end of rnd—50 sts.

Rnds 14–15: Knit.

Rnd 16: K3, M1, k11, M1, knit to end of rnd—52 sts.

Rnds 17–18: Knit.

Rnd 19: K3, M1, k13, M1, knit to end of rnd—54 sts.

Rnds 20–21: Knit.

Next rnd: K3, remove next 15 thumb sts to a stitch holder, CO 3 st onto right-hand needle, knit to end of rnd—42 sts.

Left Hand

Rnd 1: Knit to last 4 sts of rnd, pm, M1, k1, M1, knit last 3 sts of rnd—42 sts.

Rnds 2–3: Knit.

Rnd 4: Knit to marker, M1, k3, M1, k3—44 sts.

Rnds 5–6: Knit.

Rnd 7: Knit to marker, M1, k5, M1, k3—46 sts.

Rnds 8–9: Knit.

Rnd 10: Knit to marker, M1, k7, M1, k3—48 sts.

Rnds 11–12: Knit.

Rnd 13: Knit to marker, M1, k9, M1, k3—50 sts.

Rnds 14–15: Knit.

Rnd 16: Knit to marker, M1, k11, M1, k3—52 sts.

Rnds 17–18: Knit.

Rnd 19: Knit to marker, M1, k13, M1, k3—54 sts.

Rnds 20–21: Knit.

Next rnd: Knit to marker, remove marker, and move next 15 thumb sts to a stitch holder, CO 3 sts onto right-hand needle, knit to end of rnd—42 sts.

Main Mitten

Next rnd: Knit, inc 2 sts evenly—44 sts.

Knit 18 rnds (approx 6"/15cm from last garter st ridge rnd) or until desired length less 2"/5cm for fingertip shaping.

Top Decreases

Rnd 1: (K1, k2tog, k16, ssk, k1) twice—40 sts.

Rnd 2: Knit.

Rnd 3: (K1, k2tog, k14, ssk, k1) twice—36 sts.

Rnd 4: Knit.

Rnd 5: (K1, k2tog, k12, ssk, k1) twice—32 sts.

Rnd 6: Knit.

Rnd 7: (K1, k2tog, k10, ssk, k1) twice—28 sts.

Rnd 8: Knit.

Rnd 9: (K1, k2tog, k8, ssk, k1) twice—24 sts.

Rnd 10: Knit.

Rnd 11: (K1, k2tog, k6, ssk, k1) twice—20 sts.

Rnd 12: Knit.

Rnd 13: (K1, k2tog, k4, ssk, k1) twice—16 sts.

Rnd 14: Knit.

Rnd 15: (K1, k2tog, k2, ssk, k1) twice—12 sts.

Rnd 16: Knit.

Rnd 17: (K1, k2tog, ssk, k1) twice—8 sts.

Break yarn, leaving a 6"/15cm tail. Thread tail into tapestry needle and pull through rem sts. Tack down or after pulling the yarn through the sts, scoop under the st opposite the exit st, then find the nearest row of "ditches" or stitches, weave the tail down and up between the "bars" of each rnd for approx 1¼"–1½"/3cm–4cm, work back up in the opposite direction, going under where you went over previously, and over where you went under previously, for just two bars. Snip off excess.

Cuff

Unzip the crochet chain and place the 40 revealed sts onto the size 6 (4mm) dpns.

With CC2, knit 1 rnd. Purl 1 rnd. Do not break CC2.

With CC1, knit 1 rnd. Purl 1 rnd. Do not break CC1.

With MC, (k4, M1) around—50 sts.

Purl 1 rnd. Knit 1 rnd.

With size 7 (4.5mm) dpns, work 10-st rep of Winter Garden Chart for 21 rnds around for cuff. Do not break CC1 and CC2.

With MC, knit 2 rnds. Purl 1 rnd.

With CC1, knit 1 rnd. Purl 1 rnd. Break CC1.

With CC2, knit 1 rnd. Purl 1 rnd. Break CC2. With MC and size 8 (5mm) dpns, knit 5 rnds (approx¾"/2cm) for hem. BO.

With tapestry needle, sew down hem inside cuff, folding on the 2nd MC rnd for turning ridge, past the CC1 garter ridge. The CC2 turning ridge should lie flat around the cuff's lower edge.

Thumb

Place the held 15 thumb sts onto 2 dpns. With MC and size 6 (4mm) dpns, pick up and k2 sts in left thumb corner, 1 st into each of the 3 CO sts, then 1 st in last corner—21 sts.

Next rnd: K14 sts, k2tog (to close the gap that inevitably forms in this corner), k to end of rnd—20 sts.

Knit 11 rnds (approx1¾"/4.5cm).

Decreases

Rnd 1: (K2, ssk) around—15 sts.

Rnd 2: Knit.

Rnd 3: (K1, ssk) around—10 sts.

Rnd 4: (Ssk) around—5 sts.

Break yarn and end off as for fingertip shaping.

Finishing

Weave in all ends.

WINTER GARDEN MOTIF CHART

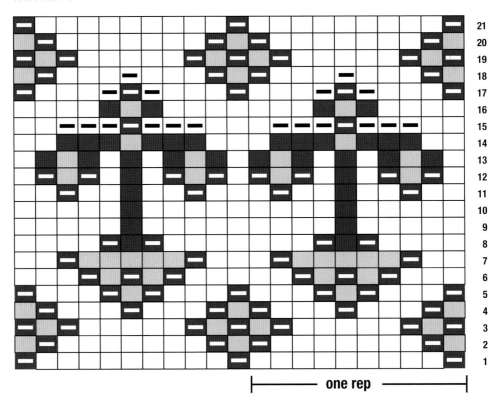

| one rep |

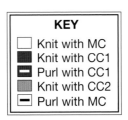

KEY
☐ Knit with MC
■ Knit with CC1
� Purl with CC1
▨ Knit with CC2
⊟ Purl with MC

ICELANDIC LEAF PATTERN TAM AND MITTENS

DESIGN BY HÉLÈNE MAGNÚSSON

From the many different types of mittens in Iceland, it is the Leaf mittens from the West Fjords that inspired me to create these mittens and matching tam. The traditional mittens, as their name suggests, were decorated with a leaf pattern. The patterns featured different types of leaves, named *fimmtekinn* (fifth), *sextekinn* (sixth), *sjötekinn* (seventh) according to the number of row repeats required to create one leaf. I used much thicker wool for the Icelandic Léttlopi, worked rather tight, to make really warm and cozy mittens. The matching tam is a new take on the tradition and is sized following the same order as the mittens. ❧

TAM

Sizes
Adult's Small (Medium, Large)

Finished Measurements
Circumference at head: 19 (21, 23)"/48.5 (53.5, 58.5)cm
Diameter across top (can be blocked larger): 9½ (10½, 11½)"/24 (26.5, 29)cm

Materials
- Léttlopi from Ístex, 100% pure Icelandic wool, 50g/1.75oz, 109yds/100m: Brown #0053 (MC), 2 (2, 3) skeins; White #0051 (CC1), 1 skein; Turquoise #1404 (CC2), 1 skein; Red #1409 (CC3),1 skein; Mustard #9264 (CC4), 1 skein; Black #0059 (CC5), 1 skein

- Sizes 4 (3.5mm) and 6 (4mm) double-pointed needles or size needed to obtain gauge

- Stitch marker

- Tapestry needle

MITTENS

Sizes
Small (Medium, Large)

Finished Measurements
Circumference around palm: 8 (8¾, 9½)"/20.5 (22, 24)cm
Length: 9 (9½, 10)"/23 (24, 25.5)cm

Materials
- Léttlopi from Ístex, 100% pure Icelandic wool, 50g/1.75oz, 109yds/100m: Brown #0053 (MC), 2 (2, 3) skeins; White #0051 (CC1), 1 skein; Turquoise #1404 (CC2), 1 skein; Red #1409 (CC3), 1 skein; Mustard #9264 (CC4), 1 skein; Black #0059 (CC5), 1 skein

- Sizes 4 (3.5mm) and 6 (4mm) double-pointed needles or size needed to obtain gauge

- Stitch markers

- Scrap yarn for thumb markers

- Tapestry needle

Gauge
20 sts and 28 rows = 4"/10cm in St st with size 6 (4mm) needles.
Adjust needle size as necessary to obtain correct gauge.

SPECIAL ABBREVIATIONS

Right leaning decrease (k2tog):
Knit 2 stitches together.

Left leaning decrease (ssk): Slip 2 stitches, one at a time as if to knit, insert left needle through the back loops and knit the two stitches together.

TAM INSTRUCTIONS

With smaller dpns and CC1, CO 96 (106, 116) sts; divide sts evenly on 3 dpns. Pm for beg of rnd and join, taking care not to twist sts. Change to MC and work 1 rnd in St st, then work in k1, p1 rib for 7 (8, 9) rnds. Change to larger dpns and St st.

Next rnd: (K4, M1) 24 times, k0 (2, 4)—120 (132,144) sts.

Cont with MC only, work 4 (5, 6) rnds. Foll chart for Pattern A for 7 rnds. Foll chart for Pattern B1 (B2, B3) for 5 (6, 7) rnds. Foll chart for Pattern C for 7 rnds.

With MC only, work 3 (4, 5) rnds.

Crown

Rnd 1: *K2, k2tog; rep from * around—90 (99, 108) sts.

Rnds 2–4: Knit.

Rnd 5: *K1, k2tog; rep from * around—60 (66, 72) sts.

With MC, work 1 (2, 3) more rnd(s).

Follow chart for Pattern D.

Change to CC5 and work 1 rnd.

Decreases

Rnd 1: *K1, k2tog; rep from * around—40 (44, 48) sts.

Rnds 2, 4, 6, and 8: Knit even.

Rnd 3: K2tog around—20 (22, 24) sts.

Rnd 5: K2tog around—10 (11, 12) sts.

Rnd 7: K2tog around—5 (6, 6) sts.

Break yarn leaving a 6"/15cm tail; draw it through the rem sts.

With tapestry needle, thread tail through rem sts, pull tight and secure to WS.

Finishing

Weave in all yarn ends. Hand wash in lukewarm water with wool soap. Block tam to measurements on circular form (for example, a plate, or a piece of cardboard covered with plastic wrap). Allow to dry flat.

MITTEN INSTRUCTIONS

With CC1 and smaller dpns, CO 40 (44, 48) sts; divide sts evenly on 3 dpns. Pm for beg of rnd and join, taking care not to twist sts. Change to MC and work 1 rnd in St st, then work in k1, p1 rib for 7 (8, 9) rnds. Change to St st. Work 1 rnd with MC, then foll chart for Pattern A for 7 rnds. Foll chart for Pattern B1 (B2, B3) for 5 (6, 7) rnds. Foll chart for Pattern C for 7 rnds. Cont with MC only for 2 rnds.

Left Thumb

Next rnd: With MC, k12 (13, 15), k next 7 (9, 9) sts with contrasting scrap yarn for thumb, place sts back on left needle and k them again with MC, k to end.

Right Thumb

Next rnd: With MC, k1, k next 7 (9, 9) sts with contrasting scrap yarn, place sts back on left needle and knit them again with MC, k to end.

Main Mitten

Cont with MC for 21 (24, 27) rnds. Foll chart for Pattern D for 7 rnds.

Change to CC5.

Next rnd: *K20 (22, 24) sts, pm; rep from * once.

Top Decreases

Next rnd: *K to last 3 sts before marker, k2tog, k2, ssk; rep from * once—36 (40, 44) sts.

Rep last rnd until 8 sts rem.

Break yarn. Turn mitten inside out and join using three-needle BO.

Thumb

Remove scrap yarn and place the sts on the needles, picking up an extra st at each of the outer corners of the thumb hole—16 (20, 20) sts.

Cont with MC for 15 (17, 19) rnds. Change to CC1 and knit 1 rnd.

Change to CC5.

Next rnd: *K8 (10, 10) sts and pm; rep from * once.

Next rnd: *K to 3 sts before first marker, k2tog, k2, ssk; rep from * once.

Rep last rnd until 8 sts rem.

Next rnd: (Ssk, k2tog) twice—4 sts.

Break yarn, leaving a 6"/15cm tail.

With tapestry needle, thread tail through rem sts, pull tight and secure to WS.

Finishing

Weave in all ends. Close the gaps at the outer corners of the thumbs if needed.

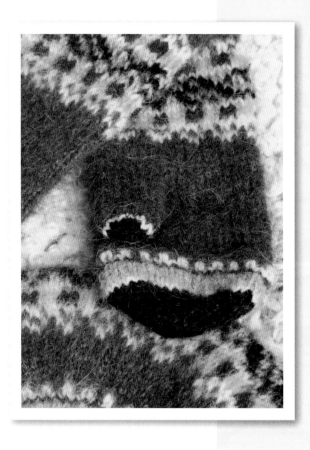

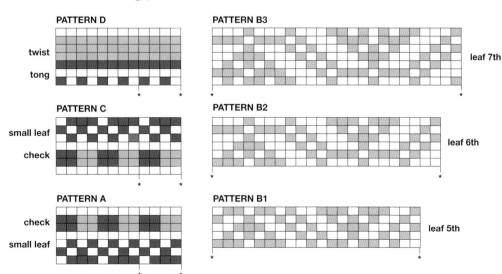

MIN ULLA HAT AND MITTENS

DESIGN BY ELINOR BROWN

These fully lined, Scandinavian-style mittens can be completed quickly due to the heavier gauge. The outer mitten features a peasant thumb, while the inner mitten has a keyhole thumb that allows the wearer to retain some thumb dexterity! ❧

HAT

Sizes
Infant/X-Small (Child/Small, Adult/Medium, Adult/Large)

Finished Measurements
Circumference at head: 14¾ (17¼, 19¾, 22¼)"/37.5 (44, 50, 56.5)cm
Length from brim to crown: 7 (7½, 8, 8½)"/18 (19, 20.5, 21.5)cm

Materials
◆ Berroco Ultra Alpaca, 50% alpaca/50% wool, 100g/3.5oz, 215yd/197m, Charcoal Mix #6289 (MC), Winter White #6201 (CC), 1 skein each
◆ Size 6 (4mm) 16"/40.5cm circular needle or size needed to obtain gauge
◆ Size 6 (4mm) double-pointed needles
◆ Stitch markers
◆ Tapestry needle

Gauge
24 sts and 26 rnds = 4"/10cm in St st with size 6 (4mm) needles.
26 sts and 26 rnds = 4"/10cm in stranded stitch pattern with size 6 (4mm) needles.
Adjust needle size as necessary to obtain correct gauge.

MITTENS

Sizes
Infant/X-Small (Child/Small, Adult/Medium, Adult/Large)

Finished Measurements
Circumference around palm: 7½ (8½, 9¾, 11)"/19 (21.5, 25, 28)cm
Length: 9½ (10½, 11¼, 11¾)"/24 (26.5, 28.5, 30)cm

Materials
◆ Berroco Ultra Alpaca, 50% alpaca/50% wool, 100g/3.5oz, 215yd/197m, Charcoal Mix #6289 (MC), Winter White #6201 (CC), 1 skein each.
◆ Size 6 (4 mm) 32 Adult /81.5cm circular needle or size needed to obtain gauge
◆ Size 6 (4mm) double-pointed needles
◆ Scrap yarn
◆ Stitch markers
◆ Tapestry needle

Gauge
24 sts and 26 rnds = 4"/10cm in St st with size 6 (4 mm) needles.
26 sts and 26 rnds = 4"/10cm in stranded stitch pattern with size 6 (4 mm) needles.
Adjust needle size as necessary to obtain correct gauge.

PATTERN NOTES

For the largest size, it may be necessary to use both the main color and the contrast color to knit the inner mitten to avoid running out of yarn. There will be plenty of both colors for the outer mitten; however, please note the inner mitten may require contrasting tips.

Important: Be sure to follow the chart for your chosen size.

HAT INSTRUCTIONS

With circular needle and CC, CO 80 (93, 106, 120) sts. Pm for beg of rnd and join, taking care not to twist sts.

Hem

Work in St st for 2 (2½, 2¾, 3)"/5 (6.5, 7, 7.5)cm. Change to MC.

Knit one rnd. Purl one rnd for turning ridge.

Next rnd: Knit, inc 16 (19, 22, 24) sts evenly across rnd—96 (112, 128, 144) sts.

Body

Follow 16-st rep of Hat Charts A, B, C, or D for 34 rnds.

Follow Chart E until hat measures 5¾ (6¼, 6½, 6¾)"/14.5 (16, 16.5, 17)cm from turning ridge.

Crown

Set-up rnd: *K12 (14, 16, 18) sts, pm; rep from * 7 times more.

Dec rnd: *K10 (12, 14, 16), k2tog, sm; rep from * 7 times more—88 (104, 120, 136) sts.

Rep dec rnd, having 1 less st between decs, every other rnd 3 (3, 4, 4) times more, then every rnd 7 (9, 10, 12) times until 8 sts rem.

Cut yarn, leaving a 6"/15cm tail. Thread a tapestry needle with the yarn tail, pull tight, and secure to WS. Thread a tapestry needle with the yarn and tack the lining to the inside of the hat.

Finishing

Weave in all ends. Block hat to smooth out color pat.

MITTEN INSTRUCTIONS

With circular needle and waste yarn, CO 48 (56, 64, 72) sts. Pm for beg of rnd and join, taking care not to twist sts. Knit one round with waste yarn.

Change to MC. Knit one round in MC.

Beg with Rnd 1 of Outer Mitten Body chart, work until Rnd 35 (41, 45, 45) has been completed.

Thumb Gusset

Left Hand

Next rnd: K16 (17, 19, 26) sts in color pat, k next 7 (9, 9, 9) sts with scrap yarn, return scrap yarn sts to left needle, k to end of rnd, working thumb sts as if they had not been knit with scrap yarn.

Right Hand

Next rnd: K1 (1, 3, 2) sts in color pat, k next 7 (9, 9, 9) sts with scrap yarn, return scrap yarn sts to left needle, k to end of rnd, working thumb sts as if they had not been knit with scrap yarn.

Both Hands

Cont to follow Outer Mitten Body chart until Rnd 52 (59, 65, 67) has been completed; at the same time, shaping top of mitten as foll:

Decreases

Dec rnd: *K1, ssk, cont in color pat to 3 sts before marker, k2tog, k1; rep from * once. Rep dec rnd every rnd 7 times more—16 (24, 32, 40) sts rem.

Cut yarn, leaving a 9"/23cm tail. Thread a tapestry needle with the yarn tail and graft rem sts tog.

Thumb

With circular needle and MC, pick up and k4 (2, 2, 2) sts on the right side of thumb, 7 (9, 9, 9) sts on bottom of thumb, 4 (2, 2, 2) sts on left side, and 7 (9, 9, 9) sts on top of thumb—22 sts. Pm and join. Remove scrap yarn. Rearrange sts on the dpns so that each needle has 2 (1, 1, 1) side st(s), then 7 (9, 9, 9) center sts and 2 (1, 1, 1) side st(s).

Follow Thumb Chart *for chosen size* until Rnd 13 (15, 15, 17) has been completed.

Dec rnd: *K1, ssk, k to 3 sts before end of needle, k2tog, k1; rep from * once.

Rep each dec round twice more—10 sts.

Cut yarn, leaving a 6"/15cm tail. Thread tapestry needle with the yarn tail and graft rem sts tog.

Main Mitten

With RS of Mitten palm facing, use circular needle to pick up 48 (56, 64, 72) sts of first MC rnd at cuff. Remove scrap yarn. Join MC.

Purl one rnd, dec 10 (12, 12, 14) sts across—38 (44, 52, 58) sts.

Set-up rnd: K19 (22, 26, 29), pm, k to end of rnd.

Cont in MC or CC for 32 (38, 41, 41) rnds.

Place Left Thumb

Rnd 1: K1, BO 6, k to end of rnd.

Rnd 2: K1, CO 6, k to end of rnd.

Place Right Thumb

Rnd 1: K 12 (15, 19, 22), BO 6, k to end of rnd.

Rnd 2: K12 (15, 19, 22), CO 6, k to end of rnd.

Both Thumbs

Cont in St st for 16 (17, 19, 21) rnds more.

Dec rnd: *K1, ssk, k to 3 sts before the marker, k2tog, k1; rep from * once.

Rep dec rnd every rnd 6 times more until 10 (16, 24, 30) sts rem.

Cut yarn, leaving a 9"/23cm tail. Thread tapestry needle with the yarn tail and graft rem sts tog.

Finishing

Weave in all ends. Block mitten to smooth out color pat.

MIN ULLA HAT CHARTS

CHART A

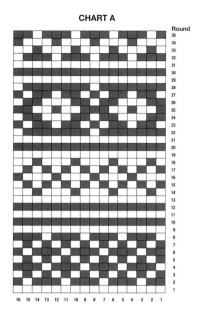

CHART B

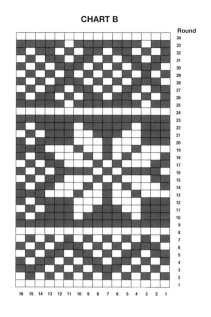

CHART C

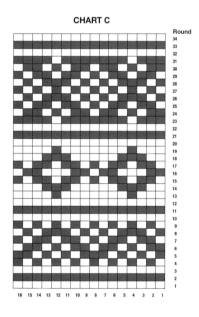

CHART D

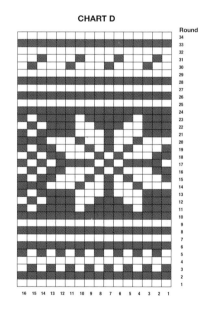

KEY
- ■ Charcoal Mix
- □ Winter White

OUTER MITTEN BODY CHART—SIZE MEDIUM

Round

THUMB CHART—SIZE MEDIUM

Round

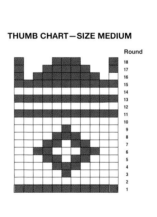

KEY

- Charcoal Mix (MC)
- Winter White (CC)
- Picked up stitch
- Right thumb placement
- Left thumb placement

OUTER MITTEN BODY CHART—SIZE SMALL

Round
68
67
66
65
64
63
62
61
60
59
58
57
56
55
54
53
52
51
50
49
48
47
46
45
44
43
42
41
40
39
38
37
36
35
34
33
32
31
30
29
28
27
26
25
24
23
22
21
20
19
18
17
16
15
14
13
12
11
10
9
8
7
6
5
4
3
2
1

THUMB CHART—SIZE SMALL

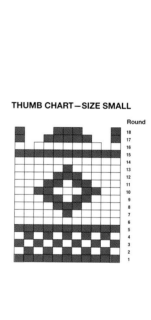

Round
18
17
16
15
14
13
12
11
10
9
8
7
6
5
4
3
2
1

KEY

- Charcoal Mix (MC)
- Winter White (CC)
- Picked up stitch
- Right thumb placement
- Left thumb placement

OUTER MITTEN BODY CHART—SIZE X-SMALL

Round
61
60
59
58
57
56
55
54
53
52
51
50
49
48
47
46
45
44
43
42
41
40
39
38
37
36
35
34
33
32
31
30
29
28
27
26
25
24
23
22
21
20
19
18
17
16
15
14
13
12
11
10
9
8
7
6
5
4
3
2
1

THUMB CHART—SIZE X-SMALL

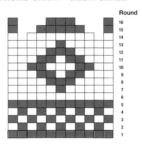

Round
16
15
14
13
12
11
10
9
8
7
6
5
4
3
2
1

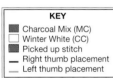

KEY
- ■ Charcoal Mix (MC)
- □ Winter White (CC)
- ■ Picked up stitch
- — Right thumb placement
- — Left thumb placement

HATS AND MITTENS OF EUROPE

LATVIAN HAT AND MITTENS

DESIGN BY LIZBETH UPITIS

Latvian myths tell of the sun leaping each morning from "Austraskoks," the sunrise tree. In these mittens, the symbol for Austra's tree—"Austras" means "sunrise"—is linked to the symbol for the sun, looking like a sunflower to our eyes.

These mittens and hat begin with a twisted edging followed by two or three traditional variations of the sun symbol. May they bring you sunny hours—both as you knit them and when you wear them. ❧

HAT

Size
Women's Average

Finished Measurements
Circumference at head: Approx. 22"/56cm
Length: Approx. 9"/23cm

Materials
- Satakieli yarn (HelmiVuorelmaOy, Finland), 100% wool, 3.5oz/100g, 360yds/329m, Green #873 (A), Gold #184 (B), Red #491 (C), and Purple #596 (D), 1 skein each
- Two size 2 (2.75mm), 16"/40.5cm circular needles or size needed to obtain gauge
- Size 3 (3.25mm) 16"/40.5cm circular needle
- Stitch marker
- Tapestry needle

Gauge
33 sts and 36 rnds = 4"/10 cm in St st with size 2 (2.75mm) needle.
Adjust needle size as necessary to obtain correct gauge.

MITTENS

Size
Women's Average

Finished Measurements
Circumference around palm: 7½"/19cm
Length: 9"/23cm

Materials
- Satakieli yarn (HelmiVuorelmaOy, Finland), 100% wool, 3.5oz/100g, 360yds/329m, Green #873 (A), Gold #184 (B), Red #491 (C), and Purple #596 (D), 1 skein each
- Size 0 (2mm) double-pointed needles (set of 5 extra-long) or size needed to obtain gauge
- Stitch marker
- Waste yarn
- Tapestry needle

Gauge
35 sts and 38 rnds = 4"/10cm in St st.
Adjust needle size as necessary to obtain correct gauge.

HAT INSTRUCTIONS

With A, larger needle, and using backward loop (half-hitch), CO 144 sts. Do not join.

Twisted Edge

Do not distribute onto four needles; do not join. Turn.

Knit all sts, forming 1 Garter st ridge.

Change to B and knit 2 rows.

Change to C and knit 2 rows.

Change to D and knit 1 row.

Next row: With D, k3 sts. To insert twist, *hold knitting on right needle in place, straight and flat; turn all sts on left needle one full turn around needle (turning away and over the top of the needle, making sure the twist does not invert sts on right needle), k6*; rep from * to *, ending k3.

Pm and join. Change to smaller needle.

With D, knit 1 rnd.

Next rnd: *K6, M1; rep from * around—168 sts.

With outside of hat facing you, work chart Rnds 11–56.

Crown

*Pm; with D k22, k2tog; rep from * 6 times more—161 sts.

Dec rnd: *Move marker, work small 4-st Sun Chart rep across each section until 3 sts before next marker. With D, k1, k2tog, rep from * 6 times more (7 sts dec).

Rep last dec rnd until 28 sts rem (4 sts each section). **Note:** When there are too few sts for a 16"/40.5cm circular needle, change to two dpns.

Cut colors B and C, leaving a 6"/15cm tail on each.

With D only, rep dec rnd 3 times more—7 sts. Bring three cuts yarn through the center hole; secure rem 7 sts by sewing through with D.

Cut yarn, leaving a 6"/15cm tail.

Top Loop

Double ply four hat colors tog. Knot plied yarns into a loop and secure into the top center hole of hat. Thread tapestry needle with 6"/15cm D tail from hat, pull tight, and secure to WS.

Finishing

Weave in all ends and trim.

Gently steam and block the hat using a medium-size mixing bowl.

MITTEN INSTRUCTIONS

Right Mitten

With A and using backward loop (half-hitch), CO 72 sts on one dpn.

Twisted Edge: Do not distribute onto four needles; do not join. Turn.

Knit all sts, forming 1 Garter st ridge.

Change to B and knit 2 rows.

Change to C and knit 2 rows.

Change to D and knit 1 row.

Next row: With D, k3 sts. To insert twist, *hold knitting on right needle in place, straight and flat, then turn all sts on left needle one full turn around needle (turning away and over the top of the needle, making sure the twist does not invert sts on the right needle), k6*; rep from * to *, ending k3.

Cuff

With outside of mitten facing you, distribute sts onto four dpns (18 sts per needle). Pm and join.

With D, knit 2 rnds.

Follow chart through Rnd 52.

Thumb Hole

Note: Place the slight jog of the beg/end line opposite the thumb. Work across sts on Needles #1 and #2; on Needle #3 **k1, CO 16 sts onto right needle, transfer 16 sts from left needle to waste yarn, k1 st rem on left of Needle #3**; k sts on Needle #4—18 sts on each dpn.

Rep Rnds 40–53 of Chart two more times. Work Rnds 40–49 of Chart.

Note: You are in the middle of the 4th rep of the medium B sun symbol.

Top Decreases

Note: When there are too few sts to knit comfortably, change to three dpns (palm sts are on one needle, hand sts are on 2nd needle).

Dec rnd: Needles #1 and #3 K1 in pat color of rnd (B or C); with D ssk, k1, finish sts on needle; on Needles #2 and #4, work in pat until 3 sts rem, with D k1, k2tog.

Rep dec rnd until 8 sts rem (4 sts on palm and 4 sts on back).

Cut B and C yarn, leaving a 6"/15cm tail and pull both yarns to mitten center.

Next rnd: With D (k1, sl 1-k2tog-psso) twice—4 sts. Cut D, leaving a 6"/15cm tail. With tapestry needle, thread tail through rem 4 sts, pull tight, and secure to WS.

Thumb

Transfer 16 sts from waste yarn onto two dpns; pick up and twist 1 st at thumb edges and place on needle for front of thumb; at the bottom of the CO sts pick up 16 CO sts for top of thumb hole; pick up and twist 1 st at thumb edges and place on needle for back of thumb—36 sts.

Note: Because color C sun symbols circle the thumb, color C symbols rep on thumb back.

Decreases

Rnds 1–2: Work in pat.

Rnd 3: Cont in pat and at beg of Needles #1 and #3, k2tog.

Rnd 4: Cont in pat and on Needles #2 and #4, work in pat until 3 sts rem, ssk, k1—32 sts.

Cont in pat until middle of 2nd C sun symbol.

Dec rnd: Work in pat and at beg of Needles #1 and #3, k1 in pat color of rnd (B or C); with D ssk, k1; on Needles #2 and #4, work in pat until 3 sts rem, with D k1, k2tog.

Rep dec rnd until 8 sts rem.

Cut yarn, leaving a 6"/15cm tail and finish as for top of Mitten.

Left Mitten

Work as Right Mitten until Thumb Gusset.

Thumb Hole

Work in pat on Needle #1; on Needle #2 rep between *s as on Needle #3 for the Right Mitten Thumb Hole, k sts on Needles #3 and #4—18 sts on each dpn.

Work as for Left Mitten Top Decreases, Thumb, and Thumb Decreases.

Finishing

Sew in all ends behind stranded knitting.

To block mittens, line up start/finish line at mitten edge and press with a damp pressing cloth and shots of steam. Lay mittens flat to dry.

SUNRISE CHART

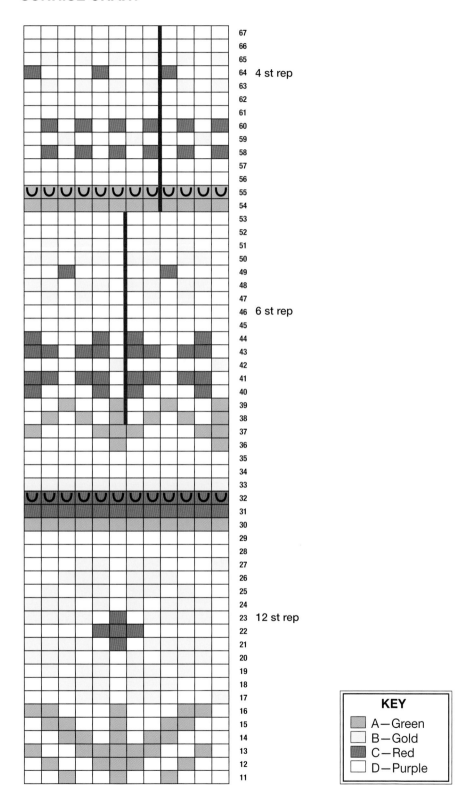

67
66
65
64 4 st rep
63
62
61
60
59
58
57
56
55
54
53
52
51
50
49
48
47
46 6 st rep
45
44
43
42
41
40
39
38
37
36
35
34
33
32
31
30
29
28
27
26
25
24
23 12 st rep
22
21
20
19
18
17
16
15
14
13
12
11

KEY

▨	A—Green
▨	B—Gold
▨	C—Red
□	D—Purple

GREEK FISHERMAN'S CAP AND GLOVES

BY ANNE CARROLL GILMOUR

Although not based on a Greek knitting tradition per se, I have always wanted to do a hand-knit version of the classic Greek fisherman's cap (I call it a Zorba cap). Matching gloves (in two adult sizes) are made with the same yarn and feature a twisted rope cable-ribbed cuff with optional braid and button trim around the top of the cuff, to reflect the braid and button trim on the cap. Both cap and gloves feature an optional anchor on the stockinette-stitch background. ❧

CAP

Sizes
Adult's Medium (Large)

Finished Measurements
Circumference at head: 21–23½"/53.5–59.5cm adjustable band
Top diameter: 9½ (10)"/24 (25.5)cm

Materials
- Cascade 220 Heathers, 100% Merino wool, 100g/3.5oz, 220yds/201m, shade # 4005, 1 skein
- Size 6 (4mm), 24"/61cm and 16"/40.5cm long circular needles or size needed to obtain gauge
- Size K/10½ (6.5mm) crochet hook
- Stitch marker
- Split-ring marker
- Tapestry needle
- Two buttons (www.buttondrawer.com item #DL190512)
- One small sheet 10-mesh plastic canvas for stiffener
- Elastic ¾"/2mm wide by 21–23"/53.5 (58.5)cm long
- Sewing thread and needle

Gauge
20 sts and 30 rows = 4"/10cm in St st
Adjust needles as necessary to obtain correct gauge.

GLOVES

Sizes
Adult's Medium (Large)

Finished Measurements
Circumference at palm: 8½ (9½)"/21.5 (24)cm
Length: 10 (10½)"/25.5 (26.5)cm

Materials
- Cascade 220 Heathers, 100% Merino wool, 100g/3.5oz, 220yds/201m, shade # 4005, 1 skein
- Size 3 (3.25mm) and 5 (3.75) double-pointed needles or size needed to obtain gauge
- Size K/10½ (6.5mm) crochet hook
- Two stitch markers
- Three stitch holders
- Tapestry needle
- Two buttons (www.buttondrawer.com item #DL190512)

Gauge
22 sts and 32 rnds = 4"/10cm in St st using size 5 (3.75mm) needles.
Adjust needles as necessary to obtain correct gauge.

SPECIAL TECHNIQUES

Edge Stitch Increases: (K1 and k1tbl) into last (edge) st or (p1 and k1tbl) into last (edge) st, which will maintain the seed stitch edge on the increase rows.

CAP INSTRUCTIONS

Using 24"/61cm long circular needle and Provisional CO, CO 19 sts (this CO edge forms the center front of the cap top and is where you will be picking up sts to work cap sides in rnd). Place a split marker around center st and work back and forth in St st with a k1 edge st at each edge as follows:

Row 1 (WS): K1 edge st, p to last 2 sts of row, p1, then (p1 and k1tbl) into last edge st (2 sts inc'd)—21 sts.

Row 2 (RS): K to last 2 sts of row, inc k1, then (k1 and k1tbl) into last edge st (2 sts inc'd)—23 sts.

Row 3: Rep Row 1—25 sts.

Row 4: Rep Row 2—27 sts.

Row 5: Rep Row 1—29 sts.

Row 6: K to last st, (k1 and k1tbl) into last st (1 st inc'd)—30 sts.

Row 7: K1, p to last st, (p1 and k1tbl) into last st (1 st inc'd)—31sts.

Row 8: Rep Row 6—32 sts.

Row 9: Rep Row 7 (1 st inc'd)—33 sts.

Row 10: Rep Row 6, inc'ing 1 st, and beg Row 1 of Anchor Chart at center st—34 sts.

Rep Rows 6 and 7 until there are 45 sts on needle; at the same time, cont top Anchor Chart. **Note:** It may be helpful to pm at each end of the center 27 motif sts.

Cont even over 45 sts as est until cap top is 8"/18cm from CO edge, ending with a WS row on Row 44 of Chart.

Decreases

Dec Row 1 (RS): Work as est to last 3 sts, k2tog, k1 (edge st)—44 sts.

Dec Row 2: Work as est to last 3 sts, p2tog, k1 (edge st)—43 sts.

Rep Dec Rows 1 and 2 until 29 sts rem, ending with Dec Row 2.

Double Dec Row 1 (RS): Work as est to last 5 sts, k2tog twice, k1 (edge st)—27 sts.

Double Dec Row 2: Work as est to last 5 sts, p2tog twice, k1 (edge st)—25 sts.

Rep Double Dec Rows 1 and 2 until 19 sts rem, ending with Double Dec Row 1.

Using 16"/40.5cm long circular needle, pick up and k under edge 38 sts p bumps to cap front CO edge, pick up and k19 sts across center front, then resume pick-up and k38 sts under p bumps down the other side of hat edge, pm for end of rnd here, then k across 19 back center sts—114 sts.

Work even for 14 rnds.

Hatband Decrease and Tuck

Dec rnd: *P6, p2tog; rep from * 13 times more, k to end of rnd—100 sts.

Next rnd: Knit even.

Tuck rnd: Pick up first p st from dec rnd above and ktog with first k st on needle, then work 2nd p st with 2nd k st, and so on to end of rnd. The hatband tuck has been completed.

Knit 10 rnds even for hatband.

Band Hem: P 1 rnd even for hem turning rnd, then k 9 rnds even for band hem.

BO loosely, leaving a 40"/101.5cm tail to whipstitch hem closed after blocking.

Brim

Using 24"/61cm circular needle and with RS of cap facing you, pick up and k13 sts across center front of hat just above p hem turning rnd. Turn and p 1 row.

Row 1 (RS): K2, M1R, pm, k9, pm, M1L, k2, pick up 2 sts from hat edge (4 sts inc'd)—17 sts.

Row 2: Turn and p to end, pick up 2 sts from hat edge—19 sts.

Row 3: K to marker, M1R, sm, k9, sm, M1L, k to end, pick up 2 sts from hat edge (4 sts inc'd)—23 sts.

Row 4: Turn and p to end, pick up 2 sts from hat edge—25 sts.

Rep Rows 3 and 4; however, pick up 3 sts on both sides twice, then 4 sts on both sides once, then 2 sts on both sides once, ending with a WS row—57 sts.

P 1 row on RS for brim edge turning row.

Brim Facing

Row 1 (WS): BO 2 sts, slipping 1st st of BO, p to end of row.

Row 2: BO 2 sts, slipping 1st st of BO, k to 2 sts before marker, ssk, sm, K9, sm, k2tog, k to end of row.

Rep last 2 rows; however, BO 4 sts at both sides, then 3 sts at both sides twice, then 2 sts at both sides twice. BO rem 13 sts on the last RS row. **Note:** The brim may appear small; however, the curvature makes it much deeper than it seems. Finished brim depth at center front should be 2"/5cm.

Finishing

Wash, then pin hatband and brim hems in place with brim stiffener inserted. Block by dressing damp cap over the narrow end of a 9"/23cm pie or tart pan (this is so the side walls and not the top get the longest stretch, which is important in achieving the classic "side wall break" that provides the distinctive look of this cap). Lay it flat, band side down, and allow to air dry completely.

Stiffen Brim

Use a template to cut plastic canvas to size of brim, trimming only if necessary. It is best if the knitting has to stretch slightly to fit over the canvas. Using a candle or match, carefully hold each edge point to the flame just long enough to melt the point into a tiny ball.

After blocking, insert stiffener in brim, then pin in place so that brim BO edge meets hat hem turning edge. Using tapestry needle and yarn tail, whipstitch brim closed.

Finish Inner Band

Measure and cut elastic to desired head circumference (21–23"/53.5–58.5cm for most adult sizes). Sew together, overlapping the ends for a flat join. Turn inner band up over elastic so that BO edge lands just under the tuck rnd. Pin in place, then, using tapestry needle and rem tail from BO, invisibly whipstitch inner band closed over elastic.

Optional: "Phoney" Hatband Seam

If you like the look of the cap as is, with a tallish crown, skip this final step. However, if you want to achieve a classic "squatty" cap silhouette, as shown in the sample, thread tapestry needle with about 36"/91.5cm length of yarn and from RS of hat, using a long running stitch, *pick up the right branch of the center back st just above the band tuck, then grab the left branch of the st just below the band tuck; rep from * around the circumference of the cap several sts at a time, maintaining normal tension. Weave in all ends.

Optional: Chain Braid and Button Trim

Using doubled sewing thread, firmly stitch buttons to hatband edge on each side where brim starts. Then using three strands of yarn held tog that are 50"/127cm in length and crochet hook, make a chain 10"/25.5cm long. Using overhand knots, make a small loop at each end with yarn tails to loop through each button, mount chain "bump" side out hiding in any yarn tails inside chain.

GLOVE INSTRUCTIONS

Cuffs

Using smaller dpns, CO 42 (48) sts. Pm for beg of rnd and join, making sure not to twist sts.

Follow Glove Cuff Chart for 3 reps plus 2 rnds (= 20 rnds), using smaller dpns for first 4 chart rnds, then change to larger dpns on Rnd 5.

Thumb Gusset Set-up

Needle #1: K17 (back of hand and anchor panel).

Left Hand

Needle #2: K16 (20).

Needle #3: K7 (8), pm to indicate beg of thumb gusset, work k1 right raised inc, k1, M1, pm to indicate end of thumb gusset, k1 (2) st(s) to end of rnd—11 (13) sts.

Note: Needle #3 will inc by 2 sts every 4th rnd until completion of thumb gusset.

Right Hand

Needle #2: K1 (2), pm to indicate beg of thumb gusset, k1 right raised inc, k1, M1, pm to indicate end of thumb gusset, k7 (8)—11 (13) sts. Move any extra sts over to Needle #3.

Needle #3: K16 (20) to end of rnd.

Both Hands

Begin foll Anchor Chart across the 17 sts on Needle #1 at Rnd 1. Cont even for 3 rnds foll Anchor Chart pat on Needle #1 as est.

On next (4th) rnd work thumb gusset incs as foll:

Thumb Gusset

On Needle #2 for right hand and Needle #3 for left hand:

Work as est to first gusset marker, sm, work a right lifted inc, k to second gusset marker, work a left lifted inc, sm (2 sts inc'd), k to end of rnd.

Cont working in this manner, completing each rnd of the Chart on Needle #1; at the same time, work the thumb gusset incs as described above every 4th round (indicated by asterisks on chart) until there are 15 sts between the two thumb gusset markers.

Cont to work even as est to desired length to base of thumb separation (about 26–30 rnds from top of cuff ribbing).

On next rnd, work even as est to first thumb gusset marker, then set aside thumb sts as foll: Remove markers as you slide all 15 sts to holder or tie onto string to keep on hold until needed to complete the thumb; CO 3 sts above thumb opening, then k rem sts of needle (**Note:** This will change total st amount to 11 [13] sts on Needle #2 for right hand or Needle #3 for left hand—44 [50] sts.)

Resume working as est until desired length to base of pinky (about 5 to 8 more rnds) and Anchor Chart is completed.

Pinky

Left Hand

On Needle #1, k16 sts, then transfer last st from Needles #1 and #2; k the next 11 (13) sts on Needle #2 for pinky, transfer rem sts onto a holder.

Right Hand

K even to last 10 (12) sts of rnd, then transfer first st from Needle #2 to Needle #3 to make a total of 11 (13) pinky sts. Transfer rem sts onto a holder.

Both Hands

Divide the 11 (13) pinky sts onto two dpns; with a third dpn, k to gap between pinky and ring finger, CO 3 sts before joining in rnds—14 (16) sts. Join and work around to tip of pinky (approx 17–20 rnds) or desired length.

K2tog across all sts. K1 rnd even.

Break yarn, leaving a 6"/15cm tail. Thread tapestry needle with tail and draw end through rem sts. Finish by invisibly weaving the end securely to inside of finger.

Ring Finger

With Needle #1, pick up and k3 sts at the base of the pinky (there are now 36 [40] hand sts total), work across next 5 (6) sts for palm for left hand *or next 5 sts from back of hand for right hand* (there are now 8 [9] sts on ring finger for left hand or 8 sts for right hand).

With Needle #2, k next 11 (13) sts.

With Needle #3, k next 12 (14) sts; sl rem sts to Needle #1 for a total of 13 (14) ring finger sts.

K1 rnd.

K3 (4) rnds or desired length over 36 (37) hand sts to base of ring finger, ending last rnd just before starting the 13 (14) ring finger sts on Needle #1. Put rem palm and back of hand sts back on holder, leaving only the ring finger sts on Needle #1.

Next rnd: K across 13 (14) ring finger sts, dividing them onto three dpn. CO 3 sts between digits sts before joining—16 (17) sts. Work 19–23 rnds or desired length to tip of ring finger.

Break yarn and finish as for pinky.

Note: You now have 23 (27) rem palm and back of hand sts on hold to finish the middle and index fingers.

Middle Finger

Reattach yarn, pick up and k3 sts at the base of the ring finger, slide the 5 sts next to the back of ring finger and the 5 (6) sts next to the palm side of ring finger off of the holders and onto two dpns, k to the area between digits, and CO 3 sts—16 (17) sts. K for 21–25 rnds or desired length.

Break yarn and finish as for pinky.

Index Finger

Reattach yarn, pick up and k3 sts at the base of the middle finger, and transfer rem 13 (15) sts from holder divided onto three dpns—16 (18) sts. K 19–23 rnds or desired length.

Break yarn and finish as for pinky.

Thumb

Transfer 15 sts from holder onto two dpns, reattach yarn, and pick up and k4 (5) sts at base of thumb opening—19 (20) sts.

K 2 (3) rnds even.

Decreases

Dec rnd: K to last st on Needle #3, ssk this st and first st from Needle #1, k to just before last pick-up st, then k2tog this last st with first st from Needle #2—17 (18) sts.

K 15–18 rnds or desired length.

Break yarn and finish as for pinky.

Finishing

Weave in all ends. Wash and block.

GREEK FISHERMAN'S CAP CHART

TOP

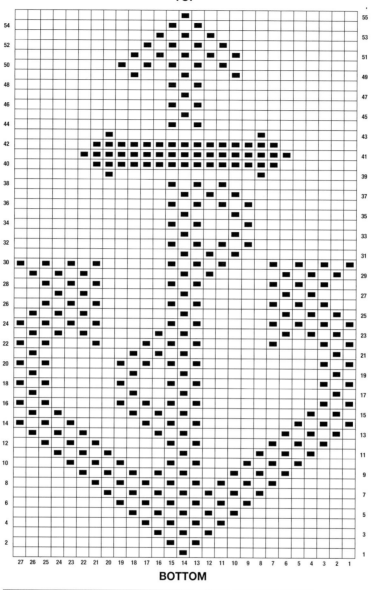

BOTTOM

KEY
■ P on right sides row, K on wrong side rows (reverse stst)
□ K on right side rows, P on wrong side rows (regular stst)

This chart is worked flat over the center 27 cap top sts for 55 rows.
Follow this chart from bottom to top, right to left on right-side rows
and left to right on wrong-side rows.

RIGHT HAND ANCHOR

LEFT HAND ANCHOR

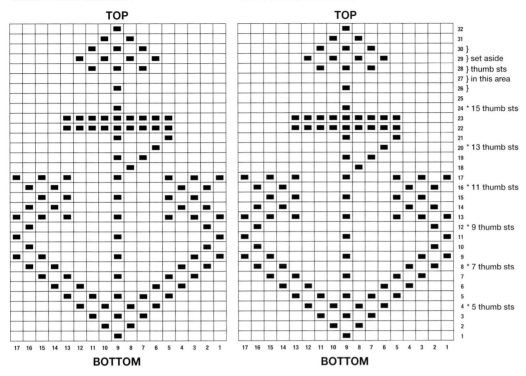

TOP

32
31
30 }
29 } set aside
28 } thumb sts
27 } in this area
26 }
25
24 * 15 thumb sts
23
22
21
20 * 13 thumb sts
19
18
17
16 * 11 thumb sts
15
14
13
12 * 9 thumb sts
11
10
9
8 * 7 thumb sts
7
6
5
4 * 5 thumb sts
3
2
1

BOTTOM

	KEY
■	P (reverse stocking st)
□	K (stocking st)

Continue working in this manner, completing each round of the chart on ndl #1 *while at the same time* working the thumb gusset increases as described above on *every 4th round (indicated by asterisks on the chart)*, until there are 15 sts between the 2 thumb gusset markers.

CUFF CHART

TOP

I	—	—	Ω	Ω	—	6
I	—	⟋⟍	⋃	≋	—	5
I	—	—	Ω	Ω	—	4
I	—	—	Ω	Ω	—	3
I	—	—	Ω	Ω	—	2
I	—	—	Ω	Ω	—	1

BOTTOM

KEY	
I	Knit (K)
—	Purl (P)
Ω	Knit 1 through back loop (K1tbl)
⟋⋃≋	Sl 2 sts on cn & hold at front, K1tbl, sl P st from cn & purl it, K1tbl last st from cn (Opt: Reverse cables for 2nd glove by holding cn at back)

Read Chart from top to bottom, right to left

LITHUANIAN CABLES AND LACE HAT AND GLOVES

DESIGN BY DONNA DRUCHUNAS

Made in a soft alpaca yarn, this set of scrumptious gloves and hat is inspired by a pair of gloves I saw in a museum in Lithuania. The originals were made in black and white, but a soft yarn and soft color scheme make the cables and lace patterns show up more and allow you to add a bit of color to your winter wardrobe. ❧

HAT

Size
Woman's Medium

Finished Measurements
Circumference at head: 24"/61cm circumference
Length: 9"/23cm

Materials
- Alpaca with a Twist, Baby Twist, 100% alpaca, 50g/1.75oz, 110 yds/101m: Berry Sorbet #3010 (MC), 2 skeins; Fireworks #2004 (CC), 1 skein
- Size 5 (3.75mm), 24"/61cm long circular needle or size needed to obtain gauge
- Size 5 (3.75mm) double-pointed needles
- Size F-5 (3.75mm) crochet hook
- Cable needle
- Stitch marker
- Tapestry needle
- Optional: Approx. ¾yd/1m, 1½"/4cm wide elastic
- Sewing needle and thread

Gauge
20 sts and 28 rnds = 4"/10cm in St st.
Adjust needle size as needed to obtain correct gauge.

GLOVES

Size
Woman's Medium

Finished Measurements
Circumference at palm: 6"/15cm
Length: 12"/30.5cm

Materials
- Alpaca with a Twist, Baby Twist, 100% alpaca, 50g/1.75oz, 110 yds/101m: Berry Sorbet #3010 (MC), 2 skeins; Fireworks #2004 (CC), 1 skein
- Size 4 (6mm) double-pointed needles or size needed to obtain gauge
- Stitch marker
- Tapestry needle

Gauge
24 sts and 32 rnds = 4"/10cm in St st.
Adjust needle size as necessary to obtain correct gauge.

HAT INSTRUCTIONS

With circular needle and MC, CO 126 sts. Pm for beg of rnd and join, taking care not to twist sts.

Hem

Work in St st until hem measures 2¾"/7cm from CO edge.

Purl 1 rnd for turning ridge.

Change to CC and knit 1 rnd.

Brim

Rnd 1: (K2tog, yo) around.

Rnd 2: K1, (k2tog, yo) to last st, k1.

Rep Rnds 1 and 2 until brim measures 3"/7.5cm.

Change to MC and knit 1 rnd.

Crown

Next rnd: K inc 12 sts evenly around—138 sts.

Begin cable pat as foll:

Rnds 1–3: (K4, P2) around.

Rnd 4: *Sl 2 sts to cn and hold in back, k2, k2 from cn, p2; rep from * around.

Rep Rnds 1–4 until hat measures approx 7"/18cm from turning ridge, ending after Rnd 4 of pat.

Decreases

Rnd 1: (K4, p2tog) around—115 sts.

Rnds 2 and 3: (K4, p1) around.

Rnd 4: *Sl 2 sts to cn and hold in back, k2, k2 from cn, p1; rep from * around.

Rnd 5: (K2tog, k2tog, p1) around—69 sts.

Rnds 6 and 7: (K2, p1) around.

Rnd 8: *Sl 1 st to cn and hold in back, k1, k1 from cn, p1; rep from * around.

Change to dpns.

Rnd 9: (K2tog, p1) around—46 sts.

Rnds 10 and 11: (K1, p1) around.

Rnd 12: Ssk around—23 sts.

Rnds 13 and 14: Knit even.

Next rnd: K2tog to last st, k—12 sts.

Last rnd: k2tog around—6 sts.

Cut yarn, leaving a 6"/15cm tail. Thread tapestry needle with yarn, pull tight, and secure to WS.

Finishing

If a tighter fit is desired, cut a piece of the elastic to fit comfortably around your head. Using the needle and sewing thread, sew the ends of the elastic together. Place the elastic inside the lace portion of the hat.

Turn up hem and stitch in place.

Weave in all ends. Wash and dry flat to block.

Tassels

With crochet hook and CC, *chain 21, single crochet in 3rd chain from hook and 2 single crochet in each rem chain. Rep from * 5 more times or until you have as many tassels as you like. Fasten off and sew tassels to top of hat.

GLOVE INSTRUCTIONS

With dpns and MC, CO 36 sts. Distribute sts evenly on three or four dpns. Pm for beg of rnd and join, taking care not to twist sts.

Hem

Work in St st until hem measures 2"/5cm.

Purl 1 rnd for turning ridge.

Change to CC and knit 1 rnd.

Cuff

Rnd 1: (K2tog, yo) around.

Rnd 2: K1, (k2tog, yo) to last st, k1.

Rep Rnds 1 and 2 until cuff measures 2¼"/5.5cm.

Change to MC and knit 1 rnd.

Inc rnd: (K4, M1) around—45 sts.

First Glove

Thumb Gusset

Rnd 1: (K4, p2) to last 3 sts, pm, k1 (thumb gusset), p2.

Rnd 2: (K4, p2) to thumb gusset, sm, M1, knit to last 2 sts, M1, p2.

Rnds 3 and 5: (K4, p2) to thumb gusset, sm, knit to last 2 sts, p2.

Rnd 4: (Sl 2 sts to cn and hold in back, k2, k2 from cn, p2) 4 times, then (k4, p2) to thumb gusset, sm, M1, knit to last 2 sts, M1, p2.

Second Glove

Thumb Gusset

Work as above, except work thumb gusset at beg of the rnd instead of at the end of the rnd, and work cable twists on last 4 sets of ribs instead of first 4.

Thumb opening

Rep Rnds 2–5 of thumb gusset until there are 13 sts in gusset. Work even until thumb gusset measures 3½"/9cm from top of cuff or reaches the web between the thumb and hand.

Put thumb sts on holder. Cont to work in pat as est, CO 4 sts over thumb opening, and return to working in-the-rnd with cables on back of hand and ribbing on palm—48 sts.

Note: You should now have 4 columns with cables on the back of the hand and 4 columns of plain ribbing on the palm.

Hand

Work even for 1½"/4cm or until knitting reaches web between pinky and ring finger.

Pinky

Put all sts on holder except on the opposite end of the rnd from the thumb; keep these 12 sts on dpns: p1, k4, p2, k4, p1. Beg working in-the-rnd on these 12 sts and CO 3 sts over gap where rem sts are on holder—15 sts total in finger, 36 sts on holder. Cont cable pat as est with p2 before and after the cable and rem sts in St st. Work even until finger measures 2"/5cm or is ¼"/6mm shorter than desired length.

Next rnd: K2tog around.

Break yarn leaving a 6"/15cm tail. Thread tapestry needle with the yarn tail, pull tight, and secure to WS.

Put sts from holder back on dpns. Work in-the-rnd and CO 3 sts over gap where pinky was—39 sts. Work 4 rnds maintaining cable and rib pat.

Ring Finger

Put all sts on holder except on the palm and back of hand just adjacent to the pinky; keep these 15 sts on dpns: p1, k4, p1 on palm, 3 sts where sts were picked up from pinky, p1, k4, p1 on back of hand, CO 3 sts over gap—18 sts in ring finger, 24 sts on holder. Cont cable pat with 2 purl sts on each side and work rem sts in St st. Work even until finger measures 2¾"/7cm or is ¼"/6mm shorter than desired length.

Next rnd: K2tog around.

Break yarn, leaving a 6"/15cm tail and fasten off as for pinky.

Middle Finger

Keep all sts on holder except on the palm and back of hand just adjacent to the pinky; keeping these 12 sts on dpns: p1, k4, p1 on palm, and p1, k4, p1 on back of hand; pick up 4 sts from ring finger and CO 4 sts over gap—20 sts in middle finger, 12 sts on holder. Cont cable pat with 2 purl sts on each side and work rem sts in St st. Work even until finger measures 3"/7.5cm or is ¼"/6mm shorter than desired length.

Next rnd: K2tog around.

Break yarn, leaving a 6"/15cm tail and fasten off as for pinky.

Index Finger

You should have 12 sts on dpns: p1, k4, p1 on palm, and p1, k4, p1 on back of hand; pick up 4 sts from ring finger—16 sts. Cont cable pat with 2 purl sts on each side and work rem sts in St st. Work even until finger measures 2¾"/7cm or is ¼"/6mm shorter than desired length.

Next rnd: K2tog around.

Break yarn, leaving a 6"/15cm tail and fasten off as for pinky.

Thumb

Put 13 thumb sts onto dpns, pick up 4 sts over gap—17 sts.

Working around in St st, k2tog at joins on first rnd—15 sts.

Work until thumb measures 1¾"/4.5cm.

Next rnd: K2tog, knit to end of rnd—14 sts.

Knit 3 rnds even.

Next rnd: K2tog around—7 sts.

Break yarn, leaving a 6"/15cm tail and fasten off as for pinky.

Finishing

Weave in ends, closing up any holes at joins between fingers.

Wash and dry flat to block.

FRENCH LACE BERET AND FINGERLESS GLOVES

DESIGN BY JENNIFER HANSEN

A feminine twist on the French classic, this lace beret features one of the simplest traditional lace patterns—Feather and Fan. Best of all, the beret requires only one skein of yarn. The wristlets are the perfect matching accessory for the hat, with knit-to-fit construction, the luxury of cashmere, and just a dash of lace or cables for elegant flair. ❧

LACE BERET

Size
One size fits all

Finished Measurements
Circumference at head: 19"/48.5cm–22"/56cm
Finished diameter at widest point: Approx 11"/28cm
(after blocking)

Materials
- Tilli Tomas Beaded Plie, 100% silk, 70g/3oz, 120yd/110m, Parchment, 1 skein (or)
- Stitch Diva Studios Studio Silk, 100% silk, 50g/2oz, 120yd/110m, Deep Fuschia, 2 skeins
- Sizes 5 (3.75mm) and 6 (4mm) double-pointed needles or two long circular needles for working in the round at small diameters
- Sizes 5 (3.75mm) and 6 (4mm) 16"/40.5cm long circular needles
- Six stitch markers
- Tapestry needle

Gauge
20 sts and 26 rows = 4"/10cm in St st with size 6 (4mm) needles.
Adjust needles as necessary to obtain correct gauge.

GAUNTLETS

Sizes
Woman's Small/Medium (Large/X-Large, XX-Large/XXX-Large)

Finished Measurements
Circumference at palm: 7½ (8, 8¾)"/19 (20.5, 22)cm
Length: 12(12, 12¾)"/30.5 (30.5, 32.5)cm

Materials
- Stitch Diva Studios *Cashmere*, 100% cashmere, 50g/1.75oz, 165yd/151m, Dove Grey (A), 1 skein
- Tilli Tomas Milan, 10% cashmere, 80% Merino wool, 10% silk, 50g/1.75oz, 165yd/151m, Dusty Pink (B), 1 skein
- Size 4 (3.5mm) double-pointed needles or size needed to obtain gauge
- Magic loop or two long circular needles for working in-the-round at small diameters
- Stitch marker
- Cable needle
- Tapestry needle

Gauge
24 sts and 28 rnds = 4"/10cm in St st.
Adjust needles as necessary to obtain correct gauge.

PATTERN NOTES

Beret is worked from the brim to the crown. A cable cast-on is worked for sturdiness and elasticity, and k1, p1 ribbing is worked for the first few rows. Work then proceeds into an increasing Feather and Fan pattern, then a decreasing pattern to the crown. A little twisted loop is worked at the top of the hat to finish.

This hat is worked in six sections. Many will find it easiest to verify work by using markers to identify each section and verifying section stitch count instead of total stitch count. Stitch counts are indicated in this pattern as follows: Total Stitch Count/Section Stitch Count.

BERET INSTRUCTIONS

With smaller circular needle, CO 96 using cable CO. Pm at beg of rnd and join, taking care not to twist sts.

Rnds 1–7: (K1, p1) around.

Change to larger circular needle.

Rnd 8–9: Work even.

Rnd 10: Note: Place markers to divide each of the 6 sections of this hat to help with st counts as work proceeds: ([K2tog] twice, [k1, yo] 8 times, [k2tog] twice, pm) 6 times (on every other rnd you will replace last pm)—120 sts/20 sts each section.

Rnd 11: Purl.

Rnds 12–13: Knit.

Rnd 14: ([K2tog] 3 times, yo, [k1, yo] 8 times, [k2tog] 3 times, sm) 6 times—138 sts/23 sts each section.

Rnds 15–17: Rep Rnds 11–13.

Rnd 18: ([K2tog] 3 times, yo, [k1, yo] 9 times, [k2tog] 4 times, sm) 6 times—156 sts/26 sts each section.

Rnd 19–21: Rep Rnds 11–13.

Rnd 22: ([K2tog] 4 times, yo, [k1, yo] 10 times, [k2tog] 4 times, sm) 6 times—174 sts/29 sts each section.

Rnd 23–25: Rep Rnds 11–13.

Rnd 26: ([K2tog] 5 times, yo, [k1, yo] 7 times, [k2tog] 6 times, sm) 6 times—156 sts/26 sts each section.

Rnds 27–29: Rep Rnds 11–13.

Rnd 30: ([K2tog] 5 times, yo, [k1, yo] 6 times, [k2tog] 5 times, sm) 6 times—138 sts/23 sts each section.

Rnd 31–33: Rep Rnds 11–13.

Rnd 34: ([K2tog] 4 times, yo, [k1, yo] 5 times, [k2tog] 5 times, sm) 6 times—120 sts/20 sts each section.

Rnd 35–37: Rep Rnds 11–13.

Rnd 38: ([K2tog] 4 times, yo, [k1, yo] 4 times, [k2tog] 5 times, sm) 6 times—102 sts/17 sts each section.

Rnd 39–41: Rep Rnds 11–13.

Rnd 42: ([K2tog] 3 times, yo, [k1, yo] 3 times, [k2tog] 4 times, sm) 6 times—84 sts/14 sts each section.

Rnd 43–45: Rep Rnds 11–13.

Rnd 46: ([K2tog] 3 times, yo, [k1, yo] twice, [k2tog] 3 times, sm) 6 times—66 sts/11 sts each section.

Rnd 47–49: Rep Rnds 11–13.

Rnd 50: ([K2tog] twice, yo, k1, yo, [k2tog] 3 times, sm) 6 times—48 sts/8 sts each section.

Rnd 51–53: Rep Rnds 11–13.

Rnd 54: ([K2tog] twice, yo, [k2tog] twice, sm) 6 times—30 sts/5 sts each section.

Rnd 55–57: Rep Rnds 11–13.

Rnd 58: ([K2tog], k1, k2tog, remove marker) 6 times—18 sts.

Rnd 59: (Sl 2 sts knitwise, knit next st, bring sl sts over knitted st) 6 times—6 sts

Cut yarn, leaving a 24"/61cm tail. Thread tail through tapestry needle and run the tail through the 6 rem sts a couple of times, then pull tightly to close the top of the hat. Weave the tail through a few sts to secure on the WS.

Beret Loop

Bring tail up through center top. Fold roughly in half in a loop that is about 8"/20.5cm tall, so that the 4"/10cm of tail remains when the bottom of the tail is pinched. Twist the two strands of the loop together until the yarn begins to twist back onto itself when folded in half and released—secure what was once the top of the loop to the hat with a tapestry needle. Twist this twist lightly once more until it twists back onto itself when folded and released, then secure the loose end of the twist to the top of the hat with a tapestry needle.

Finishing

Weave in all ends.

Block the lace, taking care as the fabric will grow substantially.

PATTERN NOTES

Gloves stretch to fit. Choose closest size based on measurement at hand just below fingers.

The wristlets are started below the elbow and worked to the wrist. The work is increased for the thumb gusset; gusset stitches are put on waste yarn while working the hands, then gusset stitches finish the thumb. Try these snug wristlets on as you go—just slip live stitches onto a long circular needle (not necessary if using magic loop) or waste yarn. Fit tips are included throughout to ensure a perfect fit.

STITCH PATTERN

Fan Shell Pattern (worked on 15 sts)

Rnd 1: K2, p11, k2.

Rnd 2: Rep Rnd 1.

Rnd 3: Ssk, k11, k2tog (2 sts dec'd).

Rnd 4: Ssk, k9, k2tog (2 sts dec'd).

Rnd 5: Ssk, k7, k2tog (2 sts dec'd).

Rnd 6: K2, (yo, k1) 5 times, yo, k2 (6 sts inc'd)—15 sts.

Rep Rnds 1–6 for Fan Shell pat.

GAUNTLET INSTRUCTIONS

CO 34 (38, 42) loosely. Pm at beg of rnd and join, taking care not to twist sts.

Rnd 1: P1 (2, 3), k2, (p1, k1) 5 times, p1, k2, p1 (3, 5), (p1, k1) 8 times, p1 (2, 3)—34 (38, 42) sts.

Rnds 2–8: Knit the knit sts and purl the p sts for 7 more rnds.

Main Fan Shell Body Set-up Rnd: P1 (2, 3), work Fan Shell pat over the next 15 sts, p2 (4, 6), k15, p1 (2, 3).

Work in est pat until 36 (36, 39) rnds or 6 (6, 6½) reps of Fan Shell pat have been completed.

Fit Tip: This point will be at the end of the wrist at the base of the hand. If you would like the wristlet to be longer or shorter, work more or fewer Fan Shell reps, ending on a full rep of Fan Shell pat for smaller two sizes, or on Rnd 3 for largest size.

Thumb Gusset

Left Gauntlet

Rnd 1: P1 (2, 3), work Fan Shell pat over next 15 sts, p2 (4, 6), k13, pm, M1R-kwise, k2, M1L-kwise, pm, p1 (2, 3)—2 sts inc'd.

Rnds 2 and 3: P1 (2, 3), work Fan Shell pat over next 15 sts, p2 (4, 6), knit the knit sts to last 1 (2, 3) st(s), sm, p1 (2, 3).

Subsequent Inc Rnds: P1 (2, 3), work Fan Shell pat over next 15 sts, p2 (4, 6), k13, sm, M1R-kwise, knit to next marker, M1L-kwise, sm, p1 (2, 3)—2 sts inc'd.

Right Gauntlet

Rnd 1: P1 (2, 3), work Fan Shell pat over next 15 sts, p2 (4, 6), pm, M1R-kwise, k2, M1L-kwise, pm, k13, p1 (2, 3)—2 sts inc'd.

Rnds 2 and 3: P1 (2, 3), work Fan Shell pat over next 15 sts, p2 (4, 6), sm, knit the knit sts and sm, p1 (2, 3).

Subsequent Inc Rnds: P1 (2, 3), work Fan Shell pat over next 15 sts, p2 (4, 6), sm, M1R-kwise, knit to next marker, M1L-kwise, sm, k13, p1 (2, 3)—2 sts inc'd.

Note: Left and Right Gauntlet Gusset

Work Right or Left Wristlet Gusset, as appropriate for a total of 24 (24, 27) rnds—16 (16, 18) sts inc'd.

Fit Tip: This point should be even with the point on your hand where the inside of the thumb meets the palm. Work more or fewer rnds of the gusset, but make sure to end with the same number of sts by working more incs (for a shorter gusset), or just working even (for a longer gusset).

Left Hand

Removing markers, p1 (2, 3), work Fan Shell pat over next 15 sts, p2 (4, 6), k13, transfer 18 (18, 20) thumb gusset sts to waste yarn without twisting, CO 2 sts using backward loop CO, p1 (2, 3).

Right Hand

Removing markers, p1 (2, 3), work Fan Shell pat over next 15 sts, p2 (4, 6), transfer 18 (18, 20) thumb gusset sts to waste yarn without twisting, CO 2 sts using backward loop CO, k13, p1 (2, 3).

Left and Right Gauntlet

Work Right or Left Hand as appropriate, then work Main Fan Shell Body Rnd for 5 more rnds (6 rnds total) for one full rep of Fan Shell. Then work 2 more rnds of Main Body Rnd, working just the first 2 rnds of Fan Shell pat.

Fit Tip: Try on at this point to make sure you like the length. Keep in mind that the ribbing will add ⅝"/15mm. You may choose to work another rep of Fan Shell pat, or to just work a longer or shorter ribbing to achieve desired length.

Next rnd: P1 (2, 3), k2, (p1, k1) 5 times, p1, k2, p1 (3, 5), (p1, k1) 8 times, p1 (2, 3)—34 (38, 42) sts.

Knit the knit sts and purl the p sts for 6 more rnds. BO.

Thumb

Transfer thumb sts from waste yarn to needles (magic loop, dpns, or two circular) and arrange across needle(s) as appropriate.

First rnd: Leaving a 10"/25.5cm starting tail with your working yarn, pick up and k4 sts at inner thumb, making sure to pick up the middle 2 sts in the 2 CO sts made when joining hand in-the-rnd above the gusset. Knit rem sts, pm, and join rnd—22 (22, 24) sts.

Knit 3 more rnds, dec 2 sts evenly in next rnd.

Fit Tip: Try on the glove while working these rnds, inc'ing or dec'ing evenly to make sure thumb is a snug fit. Make sure to end with an even number of sts and keep in mind that the ribbing will add about ⅝"/15mm of additional length.

Next rnd: Work in p1, k1 ribbing around.

Work an additional 5 rnds of p1, k1 ribbing. BO.

Finishing

Using thumb starting yarn tail, sew any holes or gaps on thumb gusset tightly from the WS. Weave in all ends.

Lightly block to stretch the lace sts on the top side of the wristlet.

ARAN ISLANDS TEAMPALL BREACHAIN HAT AND GLOVES

DESIGN BY ANNE CARROLL GILMOUR

The design for this hat was inspired by a trip to Inishmore, the largest of the three Aran Islands that are nestled in beautiful Galway Bay on the west coast of Ireland. Because this trip was taken as a wedding anniversary celebration, I began with a knit knotwork version of my wedding band—a fifteen-stitch cabled border that is worked flat and then joined in a circle, to be picked up along the seed stitch edge and completed in the round. Because this design is all about Ireland, I used Irish yarns for the samples shown here. ❧

HAT

Sizes
Adult's Small (Medium, Large)

Finished Measurements
Circumference at head: 21 (22¼, 23)"/53.5 (56.5, 58.5)cm
Length: 8 (8½, 9)"/20.5 (21.5, 23)cm

Materials
◆ **For Small Size:** Black Water Abbey Sport Weight, 100% wool, 4oz/100g, 350yds/320m, Bracken (MC), 1 skein

◆ Sublime Kid Mohair, 60% kid mohair, 35% nylon, 5% Merino wool, l.75oz/25g, 122yds/112m, Blend Shade #0023 (CC), 60yds/55m

◆ Size 3 (3.25mm), 16"/40.5cm long circular needle or size to obtain gauge

◆ Size 3 (3.25mm) double-pointed needles

◆ **For Medium Size:** Black Water Abbey Worsted Weight, 100% wool, 4oz/100g, 220yds/201m, Grey Sea (MC), 1 skein

◆ Classic Elite Inca Alpaca, 100% baby alpaca, 1.75oz/50g, 109yds/100m, Viennese Teal #1167 (CC), 60yds/55m

◆ Size 4 (3.5mm), 16"/40.5cm circular needle or size to obtain gauge

◆ Size 4 (3.5mm) double-pointed needles

◆ **For Large Size:** Kerry Woolen Mills Aran, 100% wool, 200g/8oz, 365yds/334m, Jacob, 1 skein

◆ Classic Elite Inca Alpaca, 100% baby alpaca, 1.75oz/50g, 109yds, 100m, Goucho Gray Heather #1176 (CC)

◆ Size 5 (3.75mm), 16"/40.5cm circular needle or size to obtain gauge

◆ Size 5 (3.75mm) double-pointed needles

◆ **For All Sizes:**

◆ 5 markers

◆ Cable needle

◆ Tapestry needle

Gauge
For Small Size:
24 sts and 34 rows = 4"/10cm in St st with size 3 (3.25mm) needle.

PATTERN NOTES

This pattern is for experienced knitters with good chart reading skills and an understanding of open/closed (aka knotwork) cable construction, picot hems, and reverse grafting. Because of the textural complexity of this design, the three sizes are obtained by changing gauge for each size. This hat is worked with a knotwork border, which is knit flat, joined in a ring, then picked up and knit vertically.

SPECIAL TECHNIQUES

KBB (Knit back backward): Used only on knotwork cable bases as an alternative to turning and purling back for the few stitches involved—a very handy technique for this type of open and closed knotwork cable knitting.

For Medium Size:
22 sts and 30 sts = 4"/10cm in St st with size 4 (3.5mm) needle.

For Large Size:
20 sts and 24 rows = 4"/10cm in St st with size 5 (3.75mm) needle.
Adjust needle size as necessary to obtain correct gauge.

GLOVES

Size
Adult's Small (Medium, Large)

Finished Measurements
Circumference around palm: 8 (9, 9½)"/20.5 (23, 24)cm
Length: 10 (10½, 11)"/25.5 (26.5, 28)cm

Materials
◆ **For Small Size:** Black Water Abbey Sport Weight, 100% wool, 4oz/100g, 350yds/320m, Bracken (MC), 1 skein

◆ Size 3 (3.25mm), double-pointed needle or size to obtain gauge

◆ **For Medium Size:** Black Water Abbey Worsted Weight, 100% wool, 4oz/100g, 220yds/201m, Grey Sea (MC), 1 skein

◆ Size 4 (3.5mm), 16"/40.5cm circular needle or size to obtain gauge

◆ **For Large Size:** Kerry Woolen Mills Aran, 100% wool, 200g/8oz, 365yds/334m, Jacob, 1 skein

◆ Size 5 (3.75mm), 16"/40.5cm circular needle or size to obtain gauge

For All Sizes:
◆ Cable needle

◆ Crochet hook

◆ 3 small stitch holders

◆ 4 larger stitch holders

◆ Tapestry needle

HAT INSTRUCTIONS

Border

With MC, CO 15 sts on one dpn (use a provisional CO) and leave an extra 20"/501cm tail to graft join when border is complete. Work back and forth foll Hat Border Chart #1 for 5 complete repeats of the 36-row chart.

Join: Using K&P grafting in pat as est, invisibly graft completed hat border live st end to CO end, with RS facing you to form a ring.
Note: This join will mark the beg of each rnd. (This ring may look large; however, the next pick-up rnd takes it in.)

Pick-up Rnd on Lower Edge: Using circular needle with RS of knot border ring facing you, start just above your join by sliding the needle tip under all the purl bumps around one Seed st edge. There should be about 90–92 sts on needle. Pm at joining and knit 1 rnd into your picked up sts; at the same time evenly pick up enough extra sts to total 100 sts. (**Important Note:** The goal here with pat placement is to line up 20 sts above each triple knot section of the border, so approx 1 extra st after every 9th st or so.)

P 1 rnd, k 1 rnd, p 1 rnd for Garter st.

Hat Top Chart: K 1st st tbl after rnd marker, p19, *pm, k1tbl, p19*; rep from * to * to end of rnd.

Foll Chart #2, working 20 sts at each marker (5 reps per rnd) from Rnd 1–34 (note that on Rnd 34 you will have to k2tog tbl to get to the final 5 sts).

Break off yarn, leaving a 20"/51cm tail to draw through these 5 sts and finish top with a 16-st crochet chain loop, lashing the final tail firmly several times around the base of this loop, or anchor rem tail firmly inside hat.

Hem Edge Border

Work as for pick-up rnd on lower edge.

P 1 rnd, k 1 rnd, p 1 rnd for Garter st.

K 3 rnds.

Picot Rnd: *Yo, k2tog; rep from * to end of rnd.

Hem Facing: K 3 rnds.

Break off yarn and weave tail on the last rnd.

Turn and Tack Hem

Turn the live st edge up behind your work, purl sides tog (it will fold nicely along the line of picot sts), and carefully catch the first st with its corresponding inside st and knit these tog (*do not BO*), then the 2nd live st with the 2nd st and so forth to the end of rnd, taking care to cont working st for st. If you offset any sts, your hem will twist unattractively. **Note:** Check before you cont to make sure you are back to the original 100 sts.

Liner

K even for another 3 (3.25, 3.5)"/7.5 (8.25, 9)cm more for inner liner. Beak off yarn, leaving a 60"/150cm tail. Thread tapestry needle and invisibly whipstitch the live liner sts to the upper inside edge of the border, being careful to keep the liner straight. **Note:** From the inside you can see where each wedge section begins and ends, so place each 20th st between each section. Turning the project inside-out can make this easier. This finish works better than whip stitching a BO edge because the fabric maintains good flexibility.

Finishing

Weave in all ends. Gently rinse and squeeze out any excess moisture. Block over a medium-size bowl or pot.

PATTERN NOTES

This pattern is for experienced knitters who like texture, understand open/closed (aka knotwork) cable construction, and are good chart readers. Please note that instructions that apply only to the left hand are highlighted in **bold**; those for the right hand are in *italics*. All normal text applies to both hands.

These gloves are worked with a knotwork cuff border, which is knit flat, joined in a ring, then picked up and knit vertically.

SPECIAL TECHNIQUES

KBB (Knit back backward): Used only on knotwork cable bases as an alternative to turning and purling back for the few stitches involved—a very handy technique for this type of open and closed knotwork cable knitting.

GLOVE INSTRUCTIONS

Cuff Border

With MC, CO 15 sts on one dpn (use a provisional CO) and leave an extra 20"/50.8cm tail to graft join when border is complete. Then with 2nd dpn, work back and forth foll Cuff Double-Knot Border Chart #1 for two complete repeats of the 36-row chart.

Join: Using K&P grafting in pat as est, invisibly graft completed hat border live st end to CO end, with RS facing you to form a ring. **Note:** This join will mark the beg of each rnd.

Pick-up Rnd on Lower Edge: Using circular needle with RS of knot border ring facing you, start just above your join by sliding the needle tip under all the purl bumps around one Seed st edge. You should have about 32 sts on the needle. Pm at joining and knit 1 rnd into your picked up sts; at the same time evenly pick up enough extra sts to total 40 sts.

P 1 rnd, k 1 rnd, p 1 rnd for Garter st.

Turned Picot Hem

K 3 rnds.

Picot Rnd: *Yo, k2tog; rep from * to end of rnd.

Hem Facing: K 3 rnds.

Turn and Tack Hem

Turn the live st edge up behind your work, purl sides tog (it will fold nicely along the line of picot sts), and carefully catch the first st with its corresponding inside st and knit these tog (*do not BO*), then the 2nd live st with the 2nd st and so forth to the end of rnd, taking care to cont working st for st. If you offset any sts, your hem will twist unattractively. **Note:** Check before you cont to make sure you are back to the original 40 sts.

Tip: You can slide an empty dpn under the inside cuff sts. This will help keep your hem from twisting, and you can use a third dpn to do the BO as in a standard third-needle BO.

Hand Edge Pick-up Rnd: Holding cuff with RS facing you, begin pick-up around the rem Seed st edge just to the left of the grafted seam, exactly as for hem edge. Slide needle tip (but don't knit yet) under all the purl bumps around the edge, dividing evenly on your dpns. You should again have 32 picked-up sts. K into your picked-up sts; at the same time, evenly place enough incs to total 40 sts (inc after every 4th st).

P 1 rnd, k 1 rnd, p 1 rnd.

Note: You are now ready to est hand knot panel and thumb gusset base. Remainder of glove is worked mostly in St st except for pat sts indicated on hand knot panel chart.

Hand Knot Set-up Panel:

Needle #1: Using Needle #1 (all hand knot panel sts will go on Needle #1), k2, pm on needle to indicate beg of Hand Tri-ring Knot Chart, p11, pm on needle to indicate end of Knot Chart panel chart, k2—15 sts on Needle #1.

For Left Hand Only:

Needle #2: K15.

Needle #3 (set up thumb gusset as foll):

K7, pm on needle to indicate beg of thumb gusset, k a right raised inc, k1, k a left raised inc, pm to indicate end of thumb gusset, k2—12 sts on Needle #3 (this will inc by 2 sts every 4th rnd to the end of the thumb gusset).

For Right Hand Only:

Needle #2 (set up thumb gusset as foll):

K2, pm on needle to indicate beg of thumb gusset, k a right raised inc, k1, k a left raised inc, pm on needle to indicate end of thumb gusset, k7—12 sts on Needle #2 (this number will inc by 2 sts every 4th rnd to end of the thumb gusset).

Needle #3: K15.

Beg following Knot Chart on Needle #1 at Rnd 1, then cont around for 3 rounds even as est.

On next (4th) rnd rep thumb gusset incs as indicated below:

Thumb Gusset Incs on Needle #2 for Right Hand; *on Needle #3 for Left Hand*.

Work as est to first gusset marker, sm, work a right lifted inc, k to second gusset marker, work a left lifted inc, sm—2 sts inc.

Cont working in this manner, completing each rnd of the Hand Knot Chart; at the same time, work the thumb gusset incs as described above on every 4th round (indicated by asterisks on chart) until there are 15 sts between the two thumb gusset markers.

Cont to work even until thumb gusset reaches desired length to base of the glove's thumb (2–4 more rnds or so).

On next rnd, work even as est to first thumb gusset marker, then set aside thumb sts as foll: Remove markers as you slide all 15 sts to holder or tie onto string to keep on hold until needed to complete the thumb.

CO 5 sts above thumb opening, then k rem sts of needle (this will change total st amount to 14 on *second needle for right hand* or **third needle for left hand**. Resume working as est until desired length to base of pinky (about 4–6 more rnds) or until Hand Knot Chart is completed.

Pinky

Work even as est all 15 sts on Needle #1, then for left hand only, using an empty needle, k first 12 sts on Needle #2 (slide the last 3 sts of Needle #2 onto Needle #3).

For Right Hand only, using Needle #2, k even across next 17 sts; then, with an empty needle k, the 12 sts rem from Needle #3.

Left and Right Pinkies

*Slide the 12 sts to the right end of the needle and with a second needle in your right hand, bring yarn across the back of the sts on left needle and k all 12 sts (as if making a really wide I-cord); rep from * 18–20 times or to desired length to tip of pinky.

K2 tog across 12 pinky sts—6 sts rem.

Twist crochet hook around bottom rung in the I-cord "ladder," hooking a st through all the ladder "rungs" to the tip of the pinky.

Break yarn, leaving a 6"/15cm tail. Thread tapestry needle with tail; draw tail through these rem 6 sts twice. Pull rem tail through to the inside, then lock tail into the fabric.

Main Glove

Reattach yarn and resume working hand in rnds over rem 32 sts. Beg with an empty needle, pick up and k4 sts at base of pinky (these 4 sts will become part of the ring finger—there are now 36 sts on needle); work across **next 4 sts from palm of Left Hand** or *next 5 sts from back of Right Hand*.

With another empty needle, work across next 12 sts.

With next empty needle, work next 11 sts as est.

With next empty needle, work across rem **5** or *4* sts, then also across the **8** or *9* ring finger sts (13 sts on ring finger needle—10 k sts and 3 p sts).

Cont even for 2 rnds even over these 36 sts (remembering to leave the 11 p sts as est on back of hand); stopping just before starting the 13 ring finger sts. **Note:** You are now ready to start the ring finger, but first slide all but these 13 sts onto two holders or string, then proceed as foll:

Ring Finger

Work across the 13 ring finger sts as est, dividing these sts (5, 5, 3) onto three needles. CO 3 sts between digits sts before joining; then, with the fourth empty needle, work all 16 sts in-the-rnd, keeping the 3 back-of-hand p sts in pat as est for about 22–25 rnds or desired length to the tip of finger. **Note:** Try the glove on (carefully!) to see when fingers are long enough.

K2tog across all sts on every rnd until 8 sts rem at the fingertip.

Break yarn, leaving a 6"/15cm tail. Thread tapestry needle with tail and draw end through these 8 sts. Finish by invisibly weaving the end in securely as for pinky.

Note: You should now have the 23 sts rem on holder for palm and back of hand (8 of which are p sts).

Middle Finger

Reattach yarn and pick-up and k4 sts at base of ring finger; slide the 4 p sts next to the back of ring finger and the 5 k sts next to the palm side of ring finger off of the holders and onto two dpns. Keeping the 4 back of hand sts in p, work to the area between digits and CO 3 sts. Join in-the-rnd and work these 16 sts for 23–26 rnds or desired length (this is the longest finger on most hands).

Break yarn, then finish as for ring finger.

Index Finger

Reattach yarn and pick up and k2 sts at base of middle finger, then slide the rem 14 sts from holders; divide evenly onto three dpns. Work these 16 sts in-the-rnd as for other fingers, remembering to keep the 4 p sts at back of hand in pat, to desired length (about 22–25 rnds).

Break yarn, then finish as for ring finger.

Thumb

Slide 15 sts from holder onto two dpns, then reattach yarn and with another dpn, pick up and k7 sts at base of thumb opening (Needle #1—22 sts).

Dec Rnd 1: K to last st on third dpn, then ssk this st and first st from first dpn. K to before last pick-up st, then k2tog this last st with first st from second dpn—20 sts.

K 1 rnd even.

Dec Rnd 2: Rep Dec Rnd 1—18 sts.

K 1 rnd even.

Dec Rnd 3: Rep Dec Rnd [Decrease round 1]—16 sts.

K even for 17 rnds or desired length to tip of thumb.

K2tog on every rnd until 8 sts rem.

Break yarn, leaving a 6"/15 cm tail. Thread tapestry needle with tail and draw end through these 8 sts. Pull tightly and secure on WS.

Finishing

Weave in all ends.

CHART A: HAT BORDER

TOP

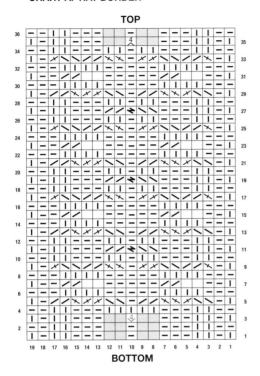

BOTTOM

Foll from bottom to top, R to L on odd numbered (RS) rows, L to R on even numbered (WS) rows.

15 sts (+ 4 then – 4 per rep) x 36 rows. Work 5 reps in total length, then after completing row 36 of 5th rep, work row 1 & 2, then join live st edge to CO edge. Remember that shaded blocks represent sts that have not yet been created or that have been decreased out.

Special note: On row 3, when this < 4 inc symbol appears, see first symbol at the top of chart key for cable base instructions.

CHART B: HAT TOP

TOP

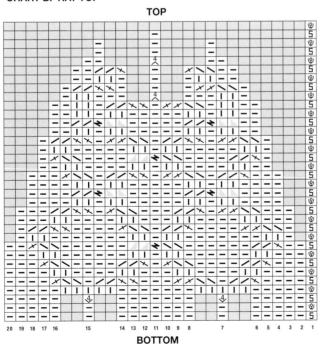

BOTTOM

Work this chart in the round, from bottom to top, right to left.

Note: On Rnd 33: P dbl dec thus: wyb, sl 2 as if to P, yf & P1, pass 2 sl sts over.

On final Rnd 34: K2tog tbl to end of rnd (only the 5 twisted knit chain sts will remain). 20 sts (+8 then -19 gradually to top) & 34 rounds, 5 repeats per rnd. Remember that shaded blocks represent stitches that either have not been created yet or stitches that once existed but have been decreased away. P2 tog decreases begin on rnd 10.

TEAMPALL BREACHAIN GLOVES CHART A: CUFF DOUBLE-KNOT

TOP

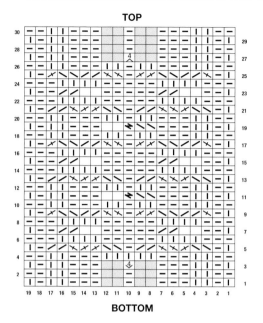

BOTTOM

Foll chart from bottom to top, R to L.

15 sts (+4 then -4) x 30 rows, worked flat for 2 complete repeats. Shaded blocks represent sts that have not yet been created or that have been decreased out.

GLOVES CHART B: HAND TRI-RING KNOT

TOP

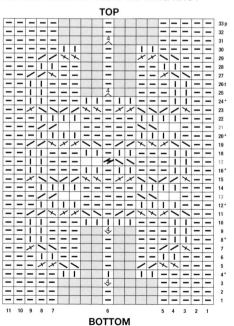

BOTTOM

KEY

⤵ Make 4 into center st cable base inc by: work 1 lifted inc to the R of central st, K central st then work an L lifted increase, then using Kbb or short row (turn work), sl 1 (as to P if turning, as to kbb if not) kbb (or P if turned) 2 sts. Finish by (working right side again now if turning…) sl 1 as to k, work 1 lifted inc R, K center st, work 1 lifted inc L, K 5th st-cable base complete. (Center st changes back to P only after increases are complete & the cable divides, as indicated on chart—it just looks smoother this way, trust me) **KBB = Knit back backward** (very handy for knotwork cable bases, bobbles, entrelac knitting, & many other applications—highly recommended for this type of open & closed knotwork cable knitting).

Ⓥ K through back loop (Ktbl).

⑤ With yarn at back, slip as to Purl (Wyb, sl as to P).

Ⅰ When working flat, K on right side, P on wrong side. In circular, K all.

– When working flat, P on right side, K on wrong side, in circular, P all.

Twist 3 L by sl 2 to cn & hold in front, P 1, K 2 from cn.

Twist 4 R by sl 2 p sts to cn & hold at back, K 2, p 2 sts from cn.

Twist 4 L by sl 2 K sts to cn & hold in front, P 2, K 2 sts from cn.

Twist 3 R by hold 1 P st at back (w/cn or fingers) K 2, P held st.

Cable 4 R by sl 2 sts to cn & hold at back, K 2, K 2 from cn.

Cable 4 L w/ P center by sl 3 sts to cn & hold in front, K 2, sl P st back to L ndl & P it, K 2 sts from cn.

Sl dec 4 sts thus: yb, sl 1st 3 sts as to P, K next 2 sts tog tbl, pass 1st 3 sl sts over st just made.

Cable 4 R w/ P center by sl 3 sts to cn & hold at back, K 2, sl P st back to L ndl & P it, K 2 sts from cn.

Foll chart from bottom to top, R to L.

11 sts (+8 then – 8) x 33 rounds. Remember that shaded blocks represent sts that have not yet been created or that have been decreased out.

*= reminder—thumb gusset increases take place every 4th rnd until round 24.

t = reminder—set aside thumb sts within the next few rnds.

p = reminder—pinky starts here.

BRITISH DRIVING CAP AND KNUCKS

DESIGN BY ANNE CARROLL GILMOUR

This Gansey-inspired British driving cap combines stitch patterning and cables from the traditional Fisherman's Gansey with the classic shape of the driving cap. The cap is easily adjustable to a custom fit, sized for adults. The cap top is knit flat, then picked up and finished in the round, and the brim is picked up and knit on last. ❦

BRITISH DRIVING CAP

Size
Adult

FINISHED MEASUREMENTS

Circumference (inner headband): 22¼"/57cm
Length from brim to center back: 14"/35.5cm

MATERIALS

- Rowan Purelife British Sheep Breeds DK, 100% wool, 50gr/3oz, 120yds/131m, Ecru Bluefaced Leicester (BFL), 2 skeins
- Size US 3 (3mm) circular needles, 16"/40.5cm and 24"/61cm long or size to obtain gauge
- Stitch markers (6)
- Split-ring markers (2)
- Tapestry needle
- Optional: Cable needle (cn)

NOTIONS

- Snap set (aka press studs) for brim
- Small sheet of 14-mesh plastic canvas to stiffen the brim
- Wide elastic, 1"/2.5cm wide and 2yds/2m long
- Covered snap set as shown, available online from www.yellowbirdfabrics.com
- Sewing needle and thread

Gauge

24 sts and 40 rows = 4"/10cm in Moss st (blocked).
Adjust needle as necessary to obtain correct gauge.

KNUCKS

Sizes
Adult's Small (Medium, Large)

FINISHED MEASUREMENTS

Circumference at palm: 6½ (7½, 8½)"/16.5 (19, 21.5)cm (blocked)
Length: 9 (9½, 10)"/23 (24, 25.5)cm

MATERIALS

- Rowan Purelife British Sheep Breeds DK, 100% wool, 50gr/3oz, 120yds/131m, Ecru Bluefaced Leicester (BFL) for Small and Medium; Brown Bluefaced Leicester (BFL) for Large, 2 skeins each
- Size US 3 (3mm) double-pointed needles (dpns) or size to obtain gauge
- Stitch markers
- Stitch holders
- Tapestry needle
- Optional: Set leather glove palms in Medium size for Small and Medium gloves; Large for Large gloves (available online from www.somersetdesigns.com/More.html)

Gauge

26 sts and 24 rows = 4"/10cm in St st (blocked).
Adjust needle size as needed to obtain correct gauge.

PATTERN NOTES

After completing chart rows and joining in rounds, center front of hat is shaped with short rows and paired decreases.

SPECIAL ABBREVIATION

w&t (wrap and turn) used on hat front brim overhang short row shaping

On knit rnds: Slip next st purlwise, yarn forward, replace slipped st back onto left needle without twisting it. Turn the work around, yarn forward, and purl back in the other direction.

On purl rnds: Slip next st purlwise, yarn back, replace slipped st back onto left needle without twisting it. Turn the work around, yarn back, and knit back in the normal direction.

SPECIAL TECHNIQUE (CAP)

Channel Island (aka "Bead") Cast-on

From the Gansey knitting tradition and a sort of cousin to the regular long-tail cast-on method. This sturdy and flexible cast-on creates an attractive row of alternating "beads" and regular stitch loops along the cast-on edge. Great for socks, gloves, and sweaters, it looks especially attractive if you are starting your project with 1x1 rib, Seed or Moss stitch, with the right side knit stitches inserted into the "bead" on the first row.

First, to make this cast-on, you need a doubled tail that is twice the length of the item you are casting on for—for instance, say you are casting on an 8" (20cm) circumference glove cuff; your doubled tail would need to be approximately 16" (40cm) long.

Start with a slipknot and pull a loop through to the desired length. Now, with slipknot on needle in your left hand, single strand from ball at back, and doubled loop in front, proceed as follows:

1. Drape the single strand attached to the ball over your left forefinger as you would for a regular long-tail cast-on. Wrap the doubled strands from the loop around your thumb two times counterclockwise and yarn over with the single strand. This yarnover will form the first stitch (after the knot.)

2. Insert needle up under the two loops on your thumb to form the "bead."

3. Pick up the single strand from forefinger as for a regular long-tail cast-on and pull this strand through the loops on your thumb. Tighten all three yarns evenly to form the beaded stitch, then begin again at step 1.

STITCH PATTERN (CAP)

Double Moss Stitch

Rnd 1 (RS): *K1, p1, rep to end of rnd.

Rnd 2: K all k sts, p all p sts.

Rnd 3: *P1, k1, rep to end of rnd.

Rnd 4: K all k sts, p all p sts.

Rep Rnds 1–4 for Double Moss st.

CAP INSTRUCTIONS

Using 24"/61cm long circular needle, CO 35 sts **Note:** CO edge becomes center front of Hat; you will eventually pick up sts along this edge, so use a CO method that you like for that purpose.

Row 1 (WS): K3, sl 1 as if to p, k2, p2, k2, p15, k2, p2, k2, sl 1 as if to p, k3.

Row 2: K1 (edge st) pm, p2, k1tbl, pm, p2, k1, M1k, k1, M1k, p2, pm, k15, pm, p2, k1, M1k, k1, M1k, p2, pm, k1tbl, p2, pm, p1, and k1 into last st (5 sts increased).

Row 3: K1 (edge st), k1, sm, k2, wyf sl 1 as to p, sm, work even as est for next 31 sts, sm, wyf sl 1 as if to p, k2, sm, p 1 and leave st on left needle, yb and k 1 tbl into same st (1 st inc).

Chart

Row 1 (RS): K1 (edge st), p1, sm, follow Chart Row 1 to last marker, sm, inc 1 as in last st on Row 3.

Row 2 and all WS rows: K1 (edge st), work even to first marker, sm, follow Chart to last marker, sm, work even to last st, inc 1 as above in last st.

Row 3 and all RS rows: K1 (edge st), work Double Moss St to first marker, sm, follow Chart to last marker, sm, work Double Moss St to last st, inc 1 as above in last st.

Cont in this manner, inc 1 k st in last st of each row until first 30-row rep of Chart has been completed. There are now 16 Double Moss sts and 1 k edge st on each side—71 sts.

Work even as est to end of 3rd chart rep, maintaining first and last st of every row in k for selvedge edge. Mark each edge of last row with split markers or contrasting yarn.

Back Shaping

Row 1 and all RS rows: K1 (edge st), work even as est to within 1 st from center, sl 2 sts tog as if to k, k1, pass 2 sl sts over (**Note:** This creates a double dec at center back that maintains the central st), work as est to last 3 sts of row, p2tog, k1 (edge st)—3 sts dec'd.

Row 2 and all WS rows: K 1 (edge st), work as est to last 3 sts, p2tog, k1 (edge st)—1 st dec'd.

Note: Discontinue the central diamond motif p sts and work all rem central motif sts in St st only, keeping cables and diminishing Double Moss sts as est.

Rep last 2 rows above until 9 Double Moss sts, cables, 1 rem central motif st, and 1 st at each edge rem—43 sts.

Work 7 rows even as est.

Note: Remainder of hat is worked in St st on front and sides with est pat across rem center back Chart sts. You will now be working these pat sts from the RS, in-the-rnd, and the 2 k edge sts can now be worked into est Double Moss st.

Hat Sides

Note: Pick up and work Hat sides in rnds, shaping center front brim overhang with short rows as foll:

Pick up and k by sliding needle tip of 16"/40.5cm long circular needle under the first 12 p bumps on the upper-left back edge to markers where decs began (remove markers); pick up and k 44 p bumps on left front edge to CO end, place first marker (left front corner); pick up and k across 27 center front sts, place second marker (right front corner); pick up and k under 44 right edge p bumps to marker where edge decs began (remove marker); pick up and k under last 12 edge p bumps, then place third marker; work chart sts as est across center back 43 sts, place fourth marker (back left corner)—182 sts.

Shaping

1st rnd: Ssk first 2 sts of rnd (back left gusset), k to 2 sts before first marker, k2tog, sm, k27 center front sts to second marker, sm, ssk, w&t; p back to first (left front corner) marker, sm, p1, w&t; k to 2 sts before third marker (back right gusset) marker, k2tog, sm, work even as est across back 43 sts to end of rnd (4 sts dec'd)—178 sts.

2nd shaping rnd: Work even to first st before the w&t from previous rnd (left front), w&t, k2tog (closing gap); k to 1 st before the w&t from previous rnd (right front), w&t, ssk (closing gap); work even as est to end of rnd (2 sts dec'd)—176 sts.

Next w&t rnd: Rep 1st shaping rnd as above, but work the right front dec 3 sts before first marker, then the left front dec 1 st after the second marker; w&t, p back to 2 sts after first (right front) marker, w&t; complete rnd as for 1st shaping rnd (4 sts dec'd)—172 sts.

Next w&t rnd: Rep 2nd shaping rnd as above (2 sts dec'd)—170 sts.

Last w&t rnd: Rep 1st shaping rnd as above, but work the right front dec 4 sts before first marker, then the left front dec 2 sts after the second marker, w&t; p back to 3 sts after first (right front) marker, w&t; complete rnd as for 1st shaping rnd above (4 sts dec'd)—166 sts.

Next rnd: Rep 2nd shaping rnd as above (2 sts dec'd)—162 sts.

Last Shaping Rnds

Rnd 1: Ssk 1st 2 sts of rnd, k to 5 sts before first marker, k2tog, k3, sm, k27 center front sts to second marker, sm, k3, ssk, k to 2 sts before third marker, k2tog, sm, work even as est across back 43 sts to end of rnd (4 sts dec'd)—158 sts.

Rnd 2: K even to 5 sts before first marker, k2tog, k3, sm, k27 center front sts to second marker, sm, K3, ssk, work even as est to end of rnd (2 sts dec'd)—156 sts.

Rep last 2 shaping rnds for 15 more rnds, having a total of 24 rnds, until there are 20 sts between Hat back and front markers on each side—112 sts.

Work even as est for 4 rnds; on last rnd k2tog at the base of each cable—110 sts.

Purl next rnd for hemline, removing all markers except one at the end of rnd.

Inner Hatband

K even all sts for 8 rnds.

Next rnd: K8, M1R, k10, M1L, k32, M1R, k10, M1L, k to end.

K 3 rnds even.

BO loosely and leave a 40"/101.5cm tail to whipstitch inner band in place after blocking.

Brim

Using 24"/61cm long circular needle and with RS facing, pick up and k15 sts across center front of hat above purl hemline and p 1 row.

Row 1 (RS): K2, M1R, pm, k11, pm, M1L, k to end of row, pick up and k2 sts from hat edge—19 sts.

Row 2: P to end of row, then pick up and p2 sts from hat edge—21 sts.

Row 3: K to marker, M1R, sm, k11, sm, M1L, k to end of row, pick up and k2 sts from hat edge—25 sts.

Row 4: P to end of row, then pick up and p2 sts from hat edge—27 sts.

Row 5: Work as for Row 3, but pick up and k3 sts from hat edge—32 sts.

Row 6: Work as for Row 4, but pick up and p3 sts from hat edge—35 sts.

Row 7: Rep Row 5 (5 sts inc'd)—40 sts.

Row 8: Rep Row 6 (3 sts inc'd)—43 sts.

Row 9: Work as for Row 3, but pick up and k4 sts from hat edge (6 sts inc'd)—49 sts.

Row 10: Work as for Row 4, but pick up and p4 sts from hat edge—53 sts.

Row 11: Rep Row 5 (5 sts inc'd)—58 sts.

Row 12: Rep Row 6 (3 sts inc'd)—61 sts.

Row 13: Rep Row 3 (5 sts inc'd)—66 sts.

Row 14: Rep Row 4 (2 sts inc'd)—68 sts.

P even 1 row for brim facing foldline.

Brim facing

Row 1: BO 2, slipping 1st st of BO, p to end of row.

Row 2: BO 2, slipping 1st st of BO, k to 2 sts before marker, ssk, sm, k11, sm, k2tog, k to end of row.

Rep last 2 rows; however, BO 4 sts at each edge once, BO 3 sts at each edge 3 more times, then 2 sts at each edge 2 times. BO rem 15 sts on last (RS) row.

Note: The brim may appear small; however, it is just right when finished.

Finishing

Wash and wet block by dressing hat over a basket, bowl, or other object with desired size/shape. The dimensions of the object should be: outer rim = 29"/73.5cm circumference, 9"/23cm cross section, 3"/7.5cm deep dome. Pin hem and brim in place and allow to dry completely.

Stiffen Brim: Use template to cut plastic canvas to size of brim. Trim if necessary as it is best if the knitting has to stretch just slightly to fit over canvas. Using a candle or match, carefully hold each edge point to the flame just long enough to melt the point into a tiny ball. Insert stiffener in brim, pin in place, but do not sew closed just yet.

Place Snaps: Pin hat front brim overhang to brim to determine and mark snap placement. Cut stabilizer using brim template and attach inside of overhang. Using strong sewing thread and needle, sew male end of snap to your mark on center of hat front brim overhang through both the knitting and the stabilizer. Sew female end of snap to your mark on the middle of top front of brim, through both knitting and canvas. Using darning needle and rem yarn tail, invisibly whipstitch brim closed.

Finish Inner Band: Turn inner band up, pin, and whipstitch in place with yarn tail.

Or

Measure and cut elastic to desired head circumference (21"/53.5cm to 23"/58.5cm) for most adult sizes). Sew together, overlapping the ends for a flat join. Turn inner band up to cover elastic and pin in place, then, using darning needle and rem tail from BO, invisibly whipstitch inner band closed over elastic.

Use the template as a general guideline, lay on your blocked and finished brim, and make any necessary adjustments before cutting plastic canvas.

PATTERN NOTES

Knucks are written using double-pointed needles; however, knitters may choose to use Magic Loop or two circular needles if desired.

Instructions that apply only to the left hand are in **bold**; those for the right hand are in *italics*. All other text applies to both hands.

Optional leather palms may be added by whipstitching into place with a small darning needle.

If you prefer full-length closed fingertips: K each digit as given to the end of each fingertip, skipping the Garter st section. Then k2tog across all sts, k 1 rnd even, then break yarn and draw end through rem sts two times. Finish by anchoring firmly and invisibly weaving the end securely to inside of finger. Note that additional yardage will be needed for full-length closed finger tips.

SPECIAL ABBREVIATIONS

Right Lifted Increase: Lift first leg of stitch below the next stitch onto needle and knit this stitch.

Left Lifted Increase: Lift last leg below last knitted stitch onto needle and knit this stitch.

STITCH PATTERNS

Double Moss Stitch (multiple of 2 sts):

Rnd 1: *K1, p1, rep from * to end of rnd.

Rnd 2: K the k sts, p the p sts.

Rnd 3: *P1, k1, rep from * to end of rnd.

Rnd 4: K the k sts, p the p sts.

Rep Rnds 1–4 for Double Moss st.

SPECIAL TECHNIQUE

Channel Island Cast-on (see page 86).

KNUCK INSTRUCTIONS

Using classic Channel Island method, CO 40 (46, 50) sts; pm for beg of rnd and join, taking care not to twist sts.

Work in Double Moss St for 8 rnds.

P 1 rnd, k 1 rnd, p 1 rnd for Garter st.

Work in k1, p1 rib for 5 rnds.

P 1 rnd, k 1 rnd, p 1 rnd for Garter st, working p2tog on last 2 sts on medium size only—40 (45, 50) sts.

Work Mock Cable Rib as foll:

Rnd 1: *K2, p1, k1tbl, p1, rep from * to end of rnd

Rnd 2: Rep Rnd 1.

Rnd 3: *K 2nd st on LH needle and leave st on needle, then k first st on LH needle, slipping both sts off needle tog, p1, k1tbl, p1, rep to end of rnd.

*Optional for second glove: Work Mock Cable cross in opposing direction on this rnd by: *k 2nd st on LH needle behind and tbl leaving st on LH needle, then k first st on LH needle and, slipping both sts off LH needle tog, p1, k1tbl, p1, rep from * to end of rnd.*

Rnd 4: Rep Rnd 1.

Rep Rnds 1–4 of Mock Cable Rib once more, then rep Rnd 1.

P 1 rnd, k 1 rnd, p 1 rnd for Garter st.

K 2 rnds even.

Thumb gusset

Needle #1: K17 (back of hand diamond panel);

Needle #2 for Left Hand only: K14 (17, 20);

Needle #3 (thumb gusset set-up for Left Hand only): K7 (8, 9), pm to indicate beg of thumb gusset, k a right raised inc, k1, k a left raised inc, pm to indicate end of thumb gusset, k1 (2, 3) to end of rnd—11 (13, 15) sts on Needle #3, which will inc by 2 sts every 4th rnd to complete thumb gusset.

Needle #2 (thumb gusset set-up for Right Hand only): K1 (2, 3), pm to indicate beg of thumb gusset, k a right raised inc, k1, k a left raised inc, pm to indicate end of thumb gusset, k7 (8, 9)—11 (13, 15) sts on Needle #2, moving any extra sts over to Needle #3.

Needle #3 for Right Hand only: K14 (17, 20) sts to end of rnd.

K 2 rnds even.

Double Moss Diamond Panel: Beg foll Diamond Panel Chart across the 17 sts on Needle #1 on Rnd 1. Cont 3 rnds even in charted pat as est.

On next rnd, work thumb gusset incs as follows on *Needle #2 for Right Hand*; **on Needle #3 for Left Hand.**

Left Hand

Work as est to first gusset marker, sm, work a right raised inc, k to second gusset marker, work a left raised inc, sm (2 sts inc'd), k to end of rnd.

Cont working in this manner, completing each rnd of the Diamond Panel Chart; at the same time work the thumb gusset incs as described above on every 4th rnd (indicated by asterisks on chart) until there are 15 sts between the two thumb gusset markers.

Cont to work even as est for 3 more rnds.

On the next rnd, work even as est to first thumb gusset marker, then set aside thumb sts as foll: Remove markers as you slide all 15 sts to holder or tie onto string to keep on hold until needed to complete the thumb; CO 4 sts above thumb opening, k rem sts on needle (**Note:** This will change total st amount to 12 (14, 16) on **Needle #2 for Right Hand;** *on Needle #3 for Left Hand*)—43 (48, 53) sts.

Resume working as est for 6–9 rnds more or until desired length to base of pinky making sure Diamond Panel Chart is completed (it is important to achieve the right depth here for a proper fit).

I-cord Pinky

For Left Hand: K first 15 (16, 16) sts on Needle #1, sl rem 2 (1, 1) st(s) off Needle #1 onto Needle #2, then k next 12 (14, 15) sts onto Needle #2 (these sts will now become the pinky). Slide any rem sts on Needle #2 onto Needle #3 for now.

For Right Hand: K all 17 sts on Needle #1. On Needle #2 k next 16 (18, 22) sts with next empty needle, k 10 (last 10 [13, 14] rem sts of rnd from Needle #3); remove rnd marker and k first 2 (2, 1) st(s) of Needle #1 onto Needle #3 (these 12 [14, 15] sts will now become the pinky).

Left and Right Hand Pinkies

*Slide these 12 (14, 15) sts to right end of needle and with a second needle in your right hand, bring yarn (fairly snug) behind sts on left needle and k all 12 (14, 15) sts. (**Note:** You are making a wide I-cord; the "ladder" should be no more than 1"/2.5cm wide.) Rep from * 12–14 times or desired length to just below second knuckle of pinky.

Work Garter st ridges cont in I-cord fashion and BO, leaving last st on needle. Now twist crochet hook around bottom rung in the I-cord ladder, hooking a st through all the ladder "rungs" to the top of the pinky. BO last st from needle with the st on crochet hook, then break off yarn. Thread tail through yarn needle to draw through rem loop and then through the first BO st to smooth out join. Invisibly weave rem tail to the inside.

Note: If you worked pinky in a circular technique, you will need to CO 1 extra st between the pinky and ring finger before joining in a circle—13 (15, 16) pinky sts.

91

Tip: Leave an extra-long tail when breaking the yarn after finishing each digit, then weave to the base of the digit just formed and use the tail to pick up and start the next digit, splicing in the ball as the tail runs out. You can also use the tail to reinforce any gaps or weak spots that may exist between digits. Skilled pick-ups eliminate this problem, but it can be very tricky to get that area just perfect, so don't be shy about using the tails for a little clean-up if you need to.

Resume hand and divide sts for ring finger—reattach yarn and cont in rnds as follows:

Starting with an empty needle, pick up and k4 sts at base of pinky (these 4 sts now start Needle #1 and will become part of the ring finger—35 [38, 42] hand sts). Add to these the 4 (5, 4) ring finger sts by working across the **next 4 (4, 6) sts from palm for Left Hand** or *next 4 (5, 5) sts from back of hand for Right Hand*—**8 (8, 10) sts on ring finger for Left Hand,** *8 (9, 9) sts for Right Hand.*

With second (empty) needle, k next 11 (12, 13) sts and sl rem sts (if any) to the next needle;

With third (empty) needle, k next 12 (13, 14) sts and sl rem sts to first (ring finger) needle for a total of 12 (13, 15) ring finger sts. Now, with empty needle, k across these ring finger sts.

K 3 (3, 4) rnds even over all 35 (38, 42) hand sts to base of ring finger, ending just before starting the 12 (13, 15) ring finger sts on Needle #1, then transfer all rem palm and back of hand sts onto string or divided onto two small holders, leaving only the ring finger sts on Needle #1.

Ring Finger

K across the 12 (13, 15) ring finger sts, dividing them onto three dpns. CO 3 sts between digits' sts before joining, then, with the fourth empty needle, work all 15 (16, 18) sts in-the-rnd for about 15–17 rnds or desired length to just below the second knuckle of finger. **Note:** Try the glove on carefully to see when fingers are long enough.

To finish Ring Finger: P 1 rnd, k 1 rnd, p1 rnd for Garter st, then BO. Break off yarn, thread tail through yarn needle to draw through the rem loop then through the first BO st to smooth out join. Anchor and invisibly weave any rem tail to the inside.

Note: There are 23 (25, 27) palm and back of hand sts on two holders to finish middle and index fingers.

Middle Finger

Reattach yarn, pick up and k3 sts at the base of the ring finger, slide the 5 sts next to back of ring finger and 5 (6, 7) sts next to palm side of ring finger off of holders and onto two dpns. K to area between digits and CO 3 sts. Join to work in-the-rnd and k these 16 (17, 18) sts for 16–18 rnds or desired length, then finish as for ring finger.

Index Finger

Reattach yarn and pick up and k3 sts at the base of the middle finger and transfer rem 13 (14, 15) held sts divided onto three dpns. Work these 16 (17, 18) sts in rnds as for other fingers to desired length (about 14–16 rounds). Finish as for other fingers.

Thumb

Transfer 15 sts from holder onto two dpns, then reattach yarn and with another dpn pick up and k4 (5, 6) sts at base of thumb opening—19 (20, 21) sts on Needle #1 for thumb. K2 (3, 4) rnds even.

Dec rnd: K to last st on third dpn, ssk this st and first st from first dpn, k to before last pick-up st, k2tog this last st with first st from second dpn—17 (18, 19) sts. K even on rem 17 (18, 19) sts to just below knuckle (9–12 rnds) or desired length. Finish as for fingers with 3 rnds. Garter st (p 1 rnd, k 1 rnd, p 1 rnd). BO. Break off yarn, thread tail through yarn needle to draw through rem loop then through the first BO st to smooth out join. Anchor securely and invisibly weave any rem tail to the inside.

Use the template below for brim stiffener and to cut stabilizer for under top snap—a thickish, soft "fleece" type is strongly suggested. It works perfectly to strengthen the fabric under the top snap while also helping the front brim overhang hold its rounded shape.

Use the templates as a general guideline—lay on your blocked and finished brim and make any necessary adjustments before cutting plastic canvas.

Templates shown at actual size.

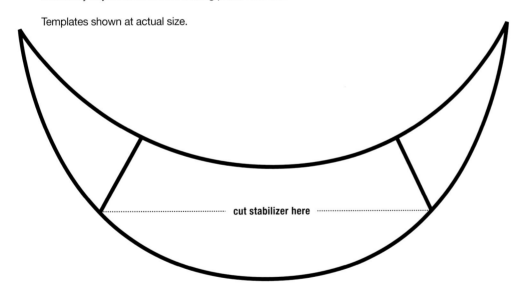

cut stabilizer here

BRITISH DRIVING CAP CHART

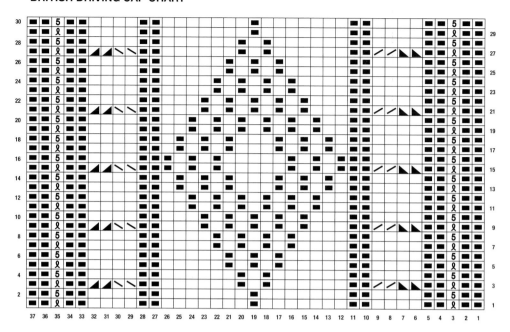

```
KEY
■  P on right side rows, K on wrong side row (reverse stocking st)
□  K on right side rows, P on wrong side rows (stocking st)
ℓ  K 1 through back lop (appears on right side rows only)
5  With yarn forward, slip 1 as to P (on wrong side rows only)
◢◥◣◤  Cable 4 Right by: sl 2 sts to cn & hold at back, K 2, K 2 sts from cn
◣◤◥◢  Cable 4 Left by: sl 2 sts to cn & hold at front, K 2, K 2 sts from cn
```

Continue in this manner, increasing 1 K st in last st of each row until 1st chart repeat is completed. There are now 16 double moss sts +1 K edge st on either side, **71 sts total**. Now work even as established, remembering to K 1st & last st of every row (maintain that all important seed st edge for later pick-up)—**to end of 3rd chart repeat.** Work to end of row 30 as established. Flag each edge of this row with split mkrs or contrasting yarn for future reference.

94

KNUCKS DIAMOND PANEL CHART

SET UP DOUBLE MOSS DIAMOND PANEL: Now begin following Diamond Panel Chart across the 17 sts on ndl #1 at round 1, cont around for **3 rounds even in charted pattern as now est.** On next **(4th)** round, again work thumb gusset inc as indicated below:

Thumb Gusset Inc on ndl #2 for right hand & ndl #3 for left hand:
Work as est to 1st gusset marker, sm, work a right lifted inc, K to 2nd gusset marker, work a left lifted inc, sm, 2sts increased. K to end of rnd.

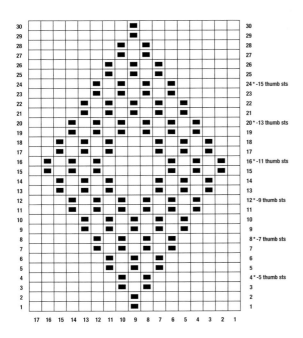

KEY
■ P (reverse stocking st)
□ K (stocking st)

Continue working in this manner, completing each round of the Diamond chart **while at the same time** working the thumb gusset increases as described above on every **4th round (indicated by asterisks on the chart)**, until there are 15 sts between the 2 thumb gusset markers.

Continue to work even as established for 3 more rounds.

HATS AND MITTENS OF THE EAST

TAI HURI-HURI HAT AND MITTS

DESIGN BY ANNE CARROLL GILMOUR

The charted designs for this New Zealand hat and mitten combo are inspired by Maori tribal creation myths, or more specifically, the Tai Huri-huri symbol, which means "Turning Tides." With the movement of the ocean as its impetus, the Tai Huri-huri symbol is said to represent the cyclical, yet ever-changing nature of life. In keeping with this theme, I chose shades that remind me of earth, sea, and sky. This design is knit in the round using Cascade 220 worsted weight 100 percent wool. ❧

HAT

Size
Adult's Medium

Finished Measurements
Circumference at head: 22"/56cm
Depth from top of crown to cast-on edge: 8½"/21.5cm

Materials
◆ Cascade 220 Heathers, 100% wool, 100g/3.75oz, 220yds/201m: #9446 Rust #9454 Lt. Grape, #2448 Dk. Blue, #9338 Dk. Green, #2452 Lt. Green, 1 skein each

◆ Cascade 220 Sport, 100% wool, 50g/1.75oz/ 164yds/150m: #8555 Black, #7807 Plum, #2404 Lt. Blue, 1 skein each

◆ Sizes 5 (3.75mm) and 7 (4.5mm) 16"/40.5cm long circular needles or size to obtain gauge

◆ Sizes 5 (3.75mm) and 7 (4.5mm) double-pointed needles

◆ Stitch marker

◆ Tapestry needle

MITTS

Size
Adult's Medium

Finished Measurements
Circumference at palm: 8"/20.5cm
Length: 9"/23cm

Materials
◆ Cascade 220 Heathers, 100% wool, 100g/3.75oz, 220yds/201m:#9446 Rust, #9454 Lt. Grape, #2448 Dk. Blue, #9338 Dk. Green, #2452 Lt. Green, 1 skein each

◆ Cascade 220 Sport, 100% wool, 50g/1.75oz/ 164yds/150m: #8555 Black, #7807 Plum, #2404 Lt. Blue, 1 skein each

◆ Sizes 5 (3.75mm) and 7 (4.5mm) 16"/40.5cm double-pointed needles or size to obtain gauge

◆ Stitch markers

◆ Tapestry needle

Gauge
22 sts and 34 rnds = 4"/10cm in St st with size 5 (3.75)mm needles.
20 sts and 32 rows = 4"/10cm in St st with size 7 (4.5)mm needles.
Adjust needles as necessary to obtain correct gauge.

PATTERN NOTES

This pattern is for skillful color knitters and good chart readers. There are never more than two shades per round, but there are frequent shade changes and long floats that should be locked back every fourth stitch. Hat is worked from bottom to top, mitts from cuff to knuckles. Charts are color-coded to correspond as closely as possible to Cascade 220 heathers and solid shades.

HAT INSTRUCTIONS

Using Black and smaller 16"/40.5 cm long circular needle, CO 100 sts. Pm at beg of rnd and join, taking care not to twist sts.

Rnds 1–3: Work in k2, p2 ribbing around.

Change to larger circular needle and work four-color chain over next 3 rnds as foll (these 3 rnds count as Rnds 1, 2, and 3 as indicated on chart):

Chain Rnd 1: Attach Lt. Green and Lt. Blue. K 1 rnd alternating the two colors to end of rnd (**Important note:** Although this is the first of the 3 rnds, it winds up in the middle [as appears on charts].)

Chain Rnd 2: Attach Rust and Lt. Grape. Bring both yarns forward as if to purl (so they are hanging outside the circle). *Holding Rust in your left hand, p1, then p1 in Lt. Grape held by your right hand*; rep from * to * to end of rnd, always bringing Rust from below and Lt. Grape from above, so that the two yarns never twist or cross each other.

Chain Rnd 3: Now change hands and complete the chain by holding Rust in the right hand (above position) and Lt. Grape in the left hand (below position) and p1 rnd (Rust into previous rnd Rust sts and Lt. Grape into previous rnd Lt. Grape sts)—chain completed.

Cont to foll Hat Chart from Rnds 4–27 for main body of hat, then rep the 3 rnds of four-color chain as above (Chart Rnds 28–30). Resume Hat Chart at Rnd 31, working double decs as indicated until only 10 sts rem. K 1 rnd even.

Break yarn, leaving a short tail. Thread tail through tapestry needle and draw through rem sts, pull tightly, and secure WS.

Finishing

Wash and block over a pot, soufflé dish or similar head-size object.

Optional braid finish: Draw 12"/30.5cm tails from last three shades used through the final opening at the top, tie in a tight overhand knot close to the hat, and braid tightly for 2"/5cm. Add beads if desired, then tie a second overhand knot and trim and comb the yarn ends.

MITT INSTRUCTIONS

Using smaller dpns and Black, CO 40 sts; divide sts evenly. Pm at beg of rnd and join, taking care not to twist sts.

Rnds 1, 2 and 3: *K2, p2; rep from * to end of rnd

Work four-color chain over the next 3 rnds as indicated by chart Rnds 1–3 as foll:

Chain Rnd 1: Attach Lt. Green and Lt. Blue. K 1 rnd alternating the two colors to end of rnd. (**Note:** Although this is the first of the 3 rnds, it winds up in the middle (as appears on charts).

Chain Rnd 2: Attach Rust and Lt. Grape. Bring both yarns forward as if to purl (so they are hanging outside the circle), *holding Rust in your left hand, p1, then p1 in Lt. Grape held by your right hand*; rep from *to* to end of rnd, always bringing Rust from below and Lt. Grape from above, so that the two yarns never twist or cross each other.

Chain Rnd 3: Change hands and complete the chain by holding Rust in the right hand (above position) and Lt. Grape in the left hand (below position) and p 1 rnd (Rust into previous rnd Rust sts and Lt. Grape into previous rnd Lt. Grape sts)—chain completed.

Rnds 4–26: Cont to foll Mitt Chart for left hand or for right hand from Rnds 4–20, then rep the 3 rnds of four-color chain as above (Chart Rnds 21–23). Change to larger needles and resume Chart at Rnd 24. Work as established until Rnd 26 has been completed.

Left Mitt

Rnd 27: Cont Left Mitt Chart over first 21 sts of Rnd 27 (back of hand sts), then work (1 black st, 1 background shade) alternating to end of rnd (palm sts).

Rnd 28: Beg thumb gusset incs as foll: Work to within last st of rnd, place first thumb gusset marker, k a right lifted inc in Lt. Blue, k1 Black st, k a left lifted inc in Lt. Blue (end of rnd marker will be second gusset marker).

Rnd 29: Work Rnd 29 as established, then rep paired thumb gusset incs in stripes as charted just after first marker and just before end of rnd marker.

Rnd 30: Work Rnd 30 as established.

Rnds 31–38: Rep paired incs as charted on all even numbered rnds to Rnd 38 (there are now 13 sts between gusset markers).

Rnd 39: Set 13 thumb sts aside as foll: Work as established to first gusset marker, remove marker as you slide all 13 sts onto a small holder for thumb, CO 1 Black st above thumb opening—40 sts.

Rnds 40–49: Cont as established.

Note: Stripes are done and color patterning resumes from Rnds 50–55 (as noted on chart).

Right Mitt

Rnd 27: Cont Right Mitt Chart as established over first 20 sts (back of hand sts), then work (1 Black st, 1 background shade) alternating to just before last st of rnd, (palm sts), then work st 40 as indicated on chart.

Rnd 28: Beg thumb gusset incs as foll: Work the first 20 sts of rnd as established, place first thumb gusset marker, k a right lifted inc in Lt. Blue, k 1 Black, k a left lifted inc in Lt. Blue, place second thumb gusset marker, k as established to end of rnd. **Rnd 29: Work even as established.**

Rnd 30: Rep thumb gusset incs as charted just after first gusset marker and just before second gusset marker.

Rnds 31–38: Cont in this manner, with paired incs as charted on even numbered rnds to Rnd 38 (there are now 13 sts between gusset markers).

Rnd 39: Set aside the 13 thumb sts as foll: Work as established to first gusset marker.

Rnd 40–49: Remove markers as you slide all 13 sts onto a small holder for thumb, then CO 1 Black st above thumb opening and cont over the 40 sts as established from Rnds 40–49.

Note: Stripes are done and color patterning resumes from Rnds 50–55 (as noted on chart).

Both Mitts

On completing color charts, break off all shades but Black. Change to smaller needles.

Next rnd: *K8, k2tog; rep to end of rnd—36 sts.

Work in k2, p2 rib for 3 rnds. BO.

Thumb

Reattach Dk. Green and Black, pick up and k3 sts above thumb opening (1 Dk. Green/1 Black/1 Dk. Green), slide sts from holder to an empty dpn, then k 1st 2 sts from holder needle onto second needle; with third (empty) needle work across the next 8 sts from holder (front) needle, then slide the last 3 sts onto pick-up (back) needle and work across (8 sts now on each needle).

Cont to work thumbs in this three-needle circular technique as foll: K across all sts on front needle alternating the two shades as already established, then turn mitt and with third (empty) needle k across all sts on back needle.

Cont thumb in this manner with 2 more rnds Black/Dk. Green, then 4 rnds Black/Dk. Blue.

Next rnd: With Black only, *k2, k2tog; rep to end of rnd—12 sts.

Work in k2, p2 rib for 3 rnds. BO.

Finishing

Weave in all ends. Use loose ends to close any gaps or spaces at the base of the thumb if needed.

Hand wash gently and dry over a vase (or similar mitt-shaped object).

TAI HURI-HURI HAT CHARTS

TOP

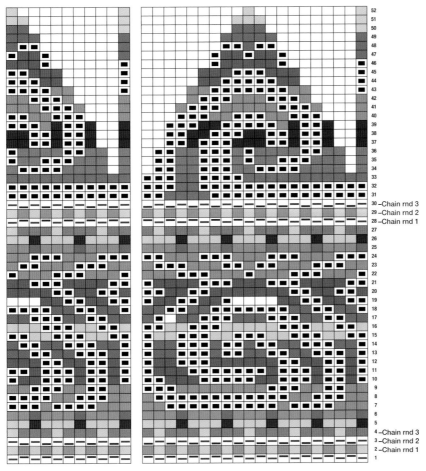

BOTTOM

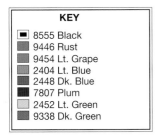

KEY

- ■ 8555 Black
- 9446 Rust
- 9454 Lt. Grape
- 2404 Lt. Blue
- 2448 Dk. Blue
- 7807 Plum
- 2452 Lt. Green
- 9338 Dk. Green

For both hat and mitts, foll charts from bottom to top, right to left.

Note on Charts: 20 sts x 53 rounds for 5 complete repeats. Chart is shown with 1 repeat & half of the following one to show positioning of double decreases (*dec rounds are also marked by asterisks), worked thus: Sl 2 as to K, K 1 pass 2 sl sts over. TIP: I find it easier to work the 1st of the 5 double decreases at the end of the round instead of the beginning (you will need to remove then replace the marker), as it eliminates the 1st & last st of the round—keep this in mind when knitting that 1st st. Shaded blocks represent sts that have been decreased away. Remember to carry long floats loosely across the back of work & lock back at least every 3rd st. Change to dp ndls when circle gets too small for circular ndl.

LEFT MITT CHART

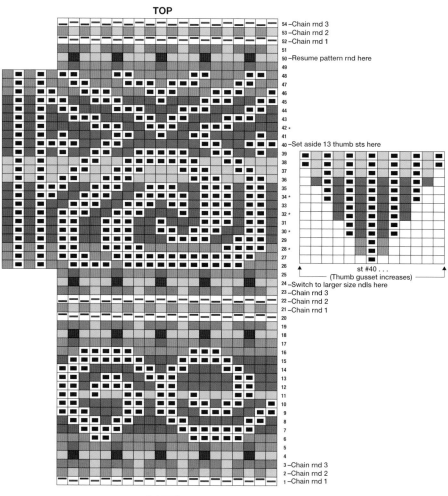

TOP

54 –Chain rnd 3
53 –Chain rnd 2
52 –Chain rnd 1
51
50 –Resume pattern rnd here
49
48
47
46
45
44
43
42 *
41
40 –Set aside 13 thumb sts here
39
38
37
36
35
34 *
33
32 *
31
30 *
29
28 *
27
26
25
24 –Switch to larger size ndls here
23 –Chain rnd 3
22 –Chain rnd 2
21 –Chain rnd 1
20
19
18
17
16
15
14
13
12
11
10
9
8
7
6
5
4
3 –Chain rnd 3
2 –Chain rnd 2
1 –Chain rnd 1

st #40 . . .
(Thumb gusset increases)

BOTTOM

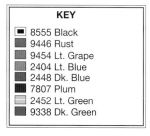

KEY	
■	8555 Black
	9446 Rust
	9454 Lt. Grape
	2404 Lt. Blue
	2448 Dk. Blue
	7807 Plum
	2452 Lt. Green
	9338 Dk. Green

Foll charts from bottom to top, right to left. Start cuff with 2 complete repeats for rnds 1–26.

1 x 1 black & background stripes on palm sts start after completing 1st 21 chart sts on rnd 27.
Color patterning all around resumes after rnd 49.

*Reminder—asterisks at rnds 28, 30, 32, 34, 36, & 38 mark paired thumb gusset increase rnds.

Rnd 40 reminder—Set aside the 13 thumb sts on rnd 40 by working 1st 39 sts of rnd as indicated on chart, place next 13 thumb sts on holder, CO 1 black st & resume rnds as established over the remaining 40 sts. (FYI: Gray squares on thumb gusset chart represent sts that have not been created yet, to more clearly indicate the paired increases for the thumb gusset.)

RIGHT MITT CHART

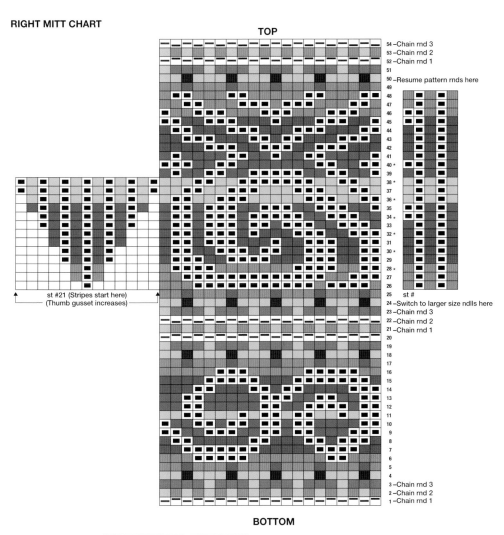

TOP

BOTTOM

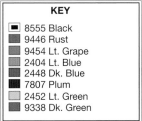

st #21 (Stripes start here)
(Thumb gusset increases)

KEY	
■	8555 Black
	9446 Rust
	9454 Lt. Grape
	2404 Lt. Blue
	2448 Dk. Blue
	7807 Plum
	2452 Lt. Green
	9338 Dk. Green

Foll charts from bottom to top, right to left.

Start cuff with 2 complete repeats for rnds 1-26.

1 x 1 black & background stripes on palm sts (except last st of round, as noted above) start after completing 1st 21 chart sts on round 27.

Color patterning all around resumes after rnd 49.

*Reminder—asterisks at rnds 28, 30, 32, 34, 36, & 38 mark paired thumb gusset increase rnds.

T= Rnd 40 reminder—Set aside the 13 sts on rnd 40 by working 1st 20 sts as est, place next 13 thumb sts on holder, CO 1 black st above opening & resume rnds as est over rem 40 sts. (FYI: Gray squares on thumb gusset chart represents sts that have not been created yet, to more clearly indicate paired increases for the thumb gusset).

JAPANESE SASHIKO HAT AND MITTENS

DESIGN BY JANEL LAIDMAN

These Sashiko mittens and hat were inspired by the beautiful Sashiko quilting tradition of Japan. Sashiko quilting uses white thread to form intricate patterns on contrasting indigo cloth. Sashiko was used as a method to reinforce the cloth as well as form decorative patterning. Our mittens and hat have the same great contrast of indigo and white in a knitted form. ❧

HAT

Size
Adult's Medium

Finished Measurements
Circumference at head: 18"/45.5cm

Materials
◆ Frog Tree Alpaca Sport, 100% alpaca, 50g/1.75oz, 230yds/119m, #000 White, 1 skein
◆ Frog Tree Alpaca Sport Melange, 50g/1.75oz, 128yds/117m, #910 Blue, 1 skein
◆ Sizes 3 (3.25mm) and 5 (3.75mm) 16"/40.5cm long circular needles or correct size to obtain gauge
◆ Stitch marker
◆ Tapestry needle

Gauge
20 sts and 32 rows = 4"/10cm in St st (blocked).
Adjust needle size as needed to obtain correct gauge

MITTENS

Size
Adult's Medium

Finished Measurements
Circumference at palm: 8"/20.5cm
Length: 10"/25.5cm

Materials
◆ Frog Tree Alpaca Sport, 100% alpaca, 50g/1.75oz, 230yds/119m, #000 White, 1 skein
◆ Frog Tree Alpaca Sport Melange, 50g/1.75oz, 128yds/117m, #910 Blue, 1 skein
◆ Size 2 (2.75mm) double-pointed needles or size to obtain gauge
◆ Stitch marker
◆ Tapestry needle

Gauge
32 sts and 36 rows = 4"/10cm in St st (blocked).
Adjust needles as necessary to obtain correct gauge.

HAT INSTRUCTIONS

Using smaller circular needle and Blue, CO 120 sts. Pm at beg of rnd and, join taking care not to twist sts.

Work in k1, p1 ribbing for 12 rnds.

K 1 rnd, inc 24 sts evenly spaced on rnd—144 sts.

Change to larger circular needle.

Join White and foll Chart 2, working shaping as indicated.

When Chart 2 is complete, break yarn, leaving a 6"/15cm tail.

Thread tapestry needle and draw yarn through rem 9 live sts, tighten, and secure to WS.

Finishing

Weave in all ends. Steam or wet block on 10¼"/26cm dinner plate.

MITTEN INSTRUCTIONS

First Mitten

Using White and dpns, CO 64 sts. Pm for beg of rnd and join, taking care not to twist sts.

Rnd 1: K.

Rnd 2: P.

Rnd 3: K.

Rnd 4: P.

Join Blue.

Rnds 5–16: Foll Chart 1 Rnds 5–16.

Rnd 17: P.

Rnd 18: K.

Rnd 19: P.

Rnd 20: K, inc 2 sts—66 sts.

Rnds 21–84: Foll Chart 1 Rnds 21–84; at the same time, at Rnd 44 create opening for thumb as indicated on chart (in red) by dropping working yarns and knitting indicated sts with waste yarn. Then drop waste yarn and cont working in pat with working yarns over waste yarn and into the rest of the rnd.

When Chart 1 is complete, close tip of mitten with Kitchener stitch.

Thumb

Return to thumb sts on waste yarn sts at the thumb opening. With White, carefully pick up sts above and below waste yarn on two needles, then snip waste yarn and remove it. When yarn is removed there are 22 live sts on your needles. Work these 22 sts in-the-rnd in St st with White until thumb is ½"/12mm less than desired length, then work as foll:

Rnd 1: *K1, ssk, k5, k2tog, k1; rep from * once—18 sts.

Rnd 2: K.

Rnd 3: *K1, ssk, k3, k2tog, k1; rep from * once—14 sts.

Rnd 4: K.

Rnd 5: *K1, ssk, k1, k2tog, k1; rep from * once—10 sts.

Close tip of thumb with Kitchener stitch.

Second Mitten

Work as for First Mitten, reversing colors (and working thumb in Blue).

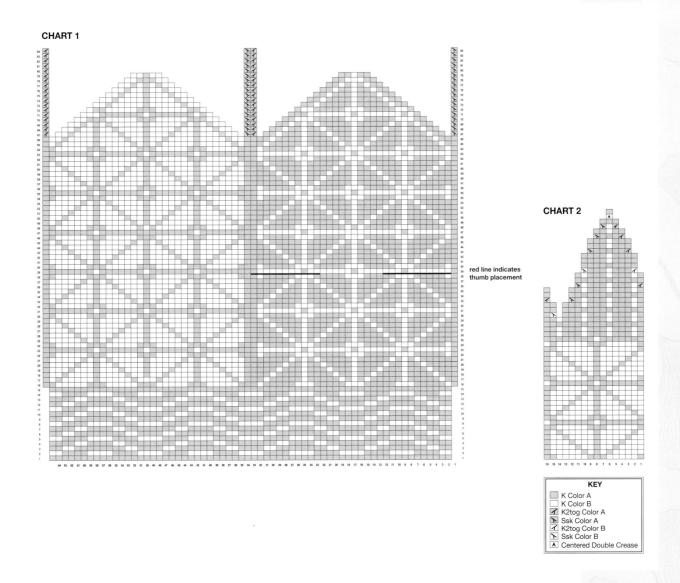

CHART 1

CHART 2

red line indicates
thumb placement

KEY	
	K Color A
	K Color B
	K2tog Color A
	Ssk Color A
	K2tog Color B
	Ssk Color B
	Centered Double Crease

CHINESE SHORT-ROW HAT AND MITTENS

DESIGN BY LILY M. CHIN

This hat design is based on the hats of ancient China, in the very traditional colors of cinnabar and black. The cinnabar is called "Terracotta," which reminds me of the soldiers in Xian. I chose to knit this set in cashmere, because more than 90 percent of all the world's cashmere fiber comes from Mongolia (though the yarn may be spun in other countries). Both the hat and the mittens are worked primarily from side to side, with short-rowed sections. This means minimal work on double-pointed needles and just one seam. ❧

HAT
Size
Adult's Average

Finished Measurements
Circumference at head: 21¾"/55cm
Length: 7"/18cm

Materials
- Lion Brand Cashmere, 100% cashmere, 88oz/25g, 82yd/75m, Terracotta #134 (A) and Onyx #153 (B), 1 skein each

- Size 5 (3.5mm) 16"/40.5cm circular needle or size needed to obtain gauge

- Size F-5 (3.75mm) crochet hook

- Stitch marker

- Tapestry needle

Gauge
22 sts and 44 rows = 4"/10cm in Garter st.
Adjust needles as necessary to obtain correct gauge.

MITTS
Size
Adult's Average

Finished Measurements
Circumference at palm: 8¾"/22cm
Length: 10"/25.5cm

Materials
- Lion Brand Cashmere, 100% cashmere, 88oz/25g, 82yd/75m, Terracotta #134 (A), 2 skeins and Onyx #153 (B), 1 skein.

- Size 5 (3.5mm) double-pointed needles or size needed to obtain gauge

- Size F-5 (3.75mm) crochet hook

- Stitch marker

- Tapestry needle

Gauge
22 sts and 44 rows = 4"/10cm in Garter st.
Adjust needles as necessary to obtain correct gauge.

HAT INSTRUCTIONS

With B and circular needle, leave at least 24"/60cm of seaming yarn tail, and work chain CO for 26 sts.

* Row 1 (WS): Sl first st with yarn in front, bring yarn to back, k24, bring yarn to front, sl last st.

Row 2 (RS): With A, k9.

Row 3: Sl first st with yarn in front, bring yarn to back, k7, bring yarn to front, sl last st. Twist colors of yarn at beg of rows to bring up other color.

Row 4: With A, k16.

Row 5: Sl first st with yarn in front, bring yarn to back, k14, bring yarn to front, sl last st. Twist colors of yarn at beg of rows to bring up other color.

Row 6: With A, k21.

Row 7: Sl first st with yarn in front, bring yarn to back, k19, bring yarn to front, sl last st. Twist colors of yarn at beg of rows to bring up other color.

Row 8: With A, k24.

Row 9: Sl first st with yarn in front, bring yarn to back, k22, bring yarn to front, sl last st. Twist colors of yarn at beg of rows to bring up other color.

Row 10: With A, k25.

Row 11: Sl first st with yarn in front, bring yarn to back, k23, bring yarn to front, sl last st. Twist colors of yarn at beg of rows to bring up other color.

Rows 12 and 13: Rep Rows 8 and 9.

Rows 14 and 15: Rep Rows 6 and 7.

Rows 16 and 17: Rep Rows 4 and 5.

Rows 18 and 19: Rep Rows 2 and 3.

Row 20: With B, k across.

Rep from * until 12 "sections" have been completed, ending with Row 19.

With long tail of B, work Row 20.

With RS still facing, pick up and knit in every other sl st at top of hat for 6 picked-up sts to gather top hole.

Place rem tail yarn onto tapestry needle and draw through last 6 picked-up sts, gather, and tie French knot. Cont to use tail and seam rem sts to beg CO.

Brim

Rnd 1: With RS facing, using B and circular needle, pick up 1 st for each sl st "chain" along lower edge of crown—120 sts.

* Rnd 2 and all even rnds: With RS still facing, p around.

Twist colors of yarn at beg of rows to bring up other color.

Rnd 3 and all odd rnds: With RS still facing, k around.

Rnds 4–8: Rep Rnds 2 and 3, ending with Rnd 2 (there are 4 B garter "ridges").

Rnd 9: With A and RS still facing, k around.

Rnd 10: With A and RS still facing, p around.

Rnd 11: With B and RS still facing, k around. *

Rep from * to * with 8 rnds of B (or 4 garter "ridges") and 2 rnds of A (or 1 garter "ridge").

End off A; work another 7 rnds of B (or 4 garter "ridges"). BO.

Finishing

Weave in all ends.

Tassel

Wrap B around 4"/10cm cardboard several times; cut bottom. Tie 6"/15cm strand around middle; fold strands in half. Tie 8"/20.5cm strand about 1"/2.5cm from folded middle and wrap a few times, then tie again. Trim bottom. Attach each end of 6"/15cm strand around middle to top of hat by knotting ends on WS.

MITT INSTRUCTIONS

Thumb

With A, chain CO 6 sts.

Row 1 and all odd rows (WS): Sl first st with yarn in front, bring yarn to back, k4, bring yarn to front, sl last st.

Row 2 (RS): K6.

Row 4 (inc row): K1, (k1, p1) in next st, k2, (p1, k1) in next st, k1—8 sts.

Rows 5–9: Rep Rows 1 and 2.

Row 10 (inc row): K1, (k1, p1) in next st, k4, (p1, k1) in next st, k1—10 sts.

Rows 11–29: Rep Rows 1–10 twice more—12 sts after Row 14, 14 sts after Row 20, 16 sts after Row 24, and 18 sts after Row 29.

Row 30: Rep Row 2.

Row 31: Rep Row 1.

Row 32: K across, divide sts onto three dpns with 6 sts per dpn, then join to form circle with RS facing.

Rnd 33: P around.

Rnd 34: K around.

Rnds 35–43: Rep Rnds 33 and 34.

Rnd 44: (Ssk, k5, k2tog) twice—14 sts.

Rnds 45–47: Rep Rnds 33 and 34.

Rnd 48: (Ssk, k3, k2tog) twice—10 sts.

Rnds 49–51: Rep Rnds 33 and 34.

Rnd 52: (Ssk, k1, k2tog) twice—6 sts.

Rnd 53: P around.

End off yarn leaving 6"/15cm tail. Place rem tail yarn onto tapestry needle and draw through last 3 sts, gather, and tie French knot.

Main Mitt

Row 1 (RS): With B, pick up and k17 sts along right side free edge of thumb or 1 st per each sl st chain, chain CO 28 sts—45 sts.

* Row 2 (WS): Sl first st with yarn in front, bring yarn to back, k43, bring yarn to front, slip last st.

Row 3 (RS): With A, k38.

Row 4: Sl first st with yarn in front, bring yarn to back, k33, bring yarn to front, sl last st. Twist colors of yarn at beg of rows to bring up other color.

Row 5: With A, k40.

Row 6: Sl first st with yarn in front, bring yarn to back, k38, bring yarn to front, sl last st. Twist colors of yarn at beg of rows to bring up other color.

Row 7: With A, k42.

Row 8: Sl first st with yarn in front, bring yarn to back, k40, bring yarn to front, sl last st. Twist colors of yarn at beg of rows to bring up other color.

Row 9: With A, k44.

Row 10: Sl first st with yarn in front, bring yarn to back, k42, bring yarn to front, sl last st. Twist colors of yarn at beg of rows to bring up other color.

Rows 11 and 12: Rep Rows 7 and 8.

Rows 13 and 14: Rep Rows 5 and 6.

Rows 15 and 16: Rep Rows 3 and 4.

Row 17: With B, k across.

Rep from * until 6 "sections" have been completed, ending with Row 17.

With RS still facing, pick up and knit in every other sl st at top of Mitt for 3 picked-up sts to gather top hole.

End off yarn, leaving 12"/30cm tail.

Place tail yarn onto tapestry needle and draw through last 3 picked-up sts, gather, and tie French knot. Cont to use tail and seam rem 28 sts to beg CO 28 sts, leaving last 17 sts free.

With WS facing, join B leaving 8"/20.5cm tail and working on rem 17 sts, sl first st with yarn in front, bring yarn to back, k15, bring yarn to front, slip last st.

Place tail yarn onto tapestry needle and seam rem 17 sts to 17 sl st chains on left side free edge of thumb.

Cuff

Rnd 1: With B and dpn and RS facing, pick up 36 sts evenly spaced around bottom edge of Mitt, about 2 sts for every 3 sl st "chains," or skip every 3rd chain.

* Rnd 2: With RS still facing, p around.

Twist colors of yarn at beg of rows to bring up other color.

Rnd 3: With RS still facing, k around.

Rnds 4–6: Rep Rnds 2 and 3, ending with Rnd 2—there are 3 B garter "ridges."

Rnd 7: With A and RS still facing, k around.

Rnd 8: With A and RS still facing, p around.

Rnd 9: With B and RS still facing, k around. *

Rep from * to *, having 6 rnds of B (or 3 garter "ridges") and 2 rnds of A (or 1 garter "ridge").

End off A, work another 5 rnds of B (or 3 garter "ridges"). BO.

Finishing

Weave in all ends.

HATS AND MITTENS OF THE WEST

Fenceline Cap and Gloves

FENCELINE CAP AND GLOVES

DESIGN BY ANNE CARROLL GILMOUR

A vintage barbed wire collection from a little cowboy museum in Kemmerer, Wyoming, served as the inspiration for the Fenceline Hat and Mittens. The vast varieties of barbed wire available to ranchers around the turn of the last century offered an array of simple but bold linear patterns that seemed to shout "knit me!" Although this is fairly easy Fair Isle–type colorwork (there are no long floats and no more than two shades per round), good two-handed color knitting and chart reading skills are helpful when knitting this design. ❧

HAT

Sizes
Child's Medium/Large (Adult's Small, Medium, Large)

Finished Measurements
Circumference at head: 20 (21, 21¾, 23)"/51 (53.5, 55, 58.5)cm
Depth: 7 (7½, 8, 8½)"/18 (19, 20.5, 21.5)cm

Materials
- Brown Sheep Nature Spun worsted weight, 100% wool, 100g/3.5oz, 345yds/315m: #601 Pepper (MC), #142W Spiced Plum (A), #522W Nervous Green (B), #124W Butterscotch (C), #225 Brick Road (D), #N59W Butterfly Blue (E), 1 skein each
- Size 5 (3.75mm) and 7 (4.5mm) 16"/40.5cm long circular needles or size needed to obtain gauge
- Size 7 (4.5mm) double-pointed needles
- Stitch markers
- Tapestry needle

Gauge
20 sts and 32 rnds = 4"/10cm in St st with size 7 (4.5mm) needles.
Adjust needles as necessary to obtain correct gauge.

MITTENS

Sizes
Child's Medium/Large (Adult's Small, Medium, Large)

Finished Measurements
Circumference at palm: 6 (7½, 8, 9)"/15 (19, 20.5, 23)cm
Length: 10 (10½, 11, 11½)"/25.5 (26.5, 28, 29)cm

Materials
- Brown Sheep Nature Spun worsted weight, 100% wool, 100g/3.5oz, 345yds/315m: #142W Spiced Plum (A), #522W Nervous Green (B), #124W Butterscotch (C), #225 Brick Road (D), #N59W Butterfly Blue (E), 1 skein each
- Sizes 5 (3.75mm) and 7 (4.5mm) double-pointed needles or size needed to obtain gauge
- Stitch marker
- Tapestry needle

Gauge
20 sts and 32 rnds = 4"/10cm in St st using size 7 (4.5mm) needles.
Adjust needles as necessary to obtain correct gauge.

PATTERN NOTES

To knit this hat with five colors instead of the "Black-top" variation shown here, eliminate the Black and use color A in its place. All other Hat samples are shown using only five colors; you will need an additional 75 yards or so of color A for the standard five-color version.

PATTERN NOTES

Fenceline Mittens in Sedona Spice colorway shown above use the same materials (but not Pepper) and chart as for the hat.

HAT INSTRUCTIONS

Using MC and smaller circular needle, CO 92 (96, 100, 108) sts. Pm at beg of rnd and join, taking care not to twist sts.

Rnds 1–3: Work in k2, p2 rib.

Change to larger circular needle and work a four-color chain over next 3 rnds as foll (break off MC as it won't be needed until chart is completed):

Chain Rnd 1: Join C and E, k 1 rnd alternating the two colors to end of rnd.

Chain Rnd 2: Join B and D, bringing both forward as if to p (so they are hanging outside the circle), *holding D in your left hand (below position) p1, then p1 in B (held by your right hand—above position)*; rep from * to * to end of rnd, always bringing D from below and B from above so that the two yarns never twist or cross each other.

Chain Rnd 3: Change hands and complete the chain by holding D in the right hand (above position) and B in the left hand (below position), then p1 rnd D into previous rnd D sts and B into previous rnd B sts—chain completed.

Foll 4-st rep of Chart for next 25 rnds. **Note:** Although there are no long floats, remember to carry yarn not in use loosely across back of work. Also asterisks at right of chart indicate thumb gusset inc rnds and do not apply to hat.

After completing Rnd 25 of Chart 1, rep the 3 rnds of 4-color purl chain exactly as at the beginning.

Crown

Reattach MC and cont with MC only.

K 1 (1, 2, 3) rnd(s), dec 2 (0, 0, 0) sts on first rnd—90 (96, 100, 108) sts.

Dec Rnd 1: *K 16 (14, 18, 16), k2tog, pm; rep from * to end of rnd, dec'ing 5 (6, 5, 6) sts—85 (90, 95, 102) sts.

K 1 rnd even.

Dec Rnd 2: *K to 2 sts before marker, k2tog, sm; rep from * to end of rnd dec'ing 5 (6, 5, 6) sts—80 (84, 90, 96) sts.

Rep Dec Rnd 2 every other rnd 4 times more—60 (60, 70, 72) sts.

Rep Dec Rnd every rnd until 5 (6, 5, 6) sts rem changing to dpns when necessary. Break off yarn, leaving a 6"/15cm tail. Thread tapestry needle and draw through rem sts, pull tightly, and secure to WS.

Finishing

Weave in all ends. Wash and block over a coffee can or similar head-size object.

MITTEN INSTRUCTIONS

Cuffs

Using A and smaller dpns, CO 32 (36, 40, 44) sts. Pm at beg of rnd and join, taking care not to twist sts.

Rnds 1–3: Work in k2, p2 rib.

Rnd 4: Join D, working k sts only in D, p sts only in A to end of rnd.

Rnd 5: Join B, working k sts only in B, p sts only in A to end of rnd.

Rnd 6: Join E, working k sts only in E, p sts only in A to end of rnd.

Rnd 7: Join C, working k sts only in C, p sts only in A to end of rnd.

Rnd 8: Rep Rnd 4.

Rnds 9–11: Using A, work 3 rnds in k2, p2 rib.

Change to larger dpns and St st, foll Chart 4-st rep for 25 rnds; at the same time work thumb gusset incs as foll (**Note:** Thumb gusset inc rnds are indicated by *s on chart and are placed to make it possible to rem in color pat):

Thumb Gusset

Work even over 32 (36, 40, 44) sts for Rnds 1–8 of chart. Beg on the 9th rnd, sl rnd marker and work 1 lifted inc to the right, then place first gusset marker; k1, then work 1 lifted inc to the left; place second thumb gusset marker, k to end of rnd—34 (38, 42, 46) sts. Work 2 more paired incs on Rnd 10 of chart (1 right leaning after first marker, 1 left leaning before second marker) There will now be 4 thumb sts between the two gusset markers—36 (40, 44, 48) sts. Cont even in pat until you have completed Rnd 14; rep paired incs as above on Rnd 15. Work Rnd 16 even, rep paired incs on Rnd 17 (8 thumb sts between the two markers)—40 (44, 48, 52) sts. Work even in pat until you have completed Rnd 23. Rep incs on Rnd 24 (10 thumb sts between the two markers)—42 (46, 50, 54) sts. K last rnd of Chart even. Break off all yarn but A, then work 2 rnds even.

For size Large only: Work 1 more set of thumb incs (12 thumb sts between the 2 markers)—56 sts. Work 1 more rnd even.

Main Mitten

Next rnd: K1, place 10 (10, 10, 12) thumb sts on a small holder removing gusset markers; CO 2 sts above thumb opening—34 (38, 42, 46) sts.

Work 1 (1, 2, 2) rnd(s) even.

On next rnd work mirror image decs above thumb as foll: K1, k2tog, k to within last 2 sts of rnd, ssk—32 (36, 40, 44) sts.

Work even until you are just past the tip of the mitten's desired length for the pinky.

Spiral Top Shaping:

Dec rnd: *K6 (7, 8, 9) sts, k2tog, pm; rep from * to end of rnd—28 (32, 36, 40) sts.

K 1 rnd even.

Next and all subsequent dec rnds: *K to 2 sts before marker, k2tog, sm; rep from * to end of rnd.

Rep last 2 rnds until only 12 sts rem.

Next rnd: K even.

Next rnd: K2tog to end of rnd—6 sts.

Break off yarn, leaving a 12"/30.5cm tail. Thread tapestry needle and draw through rem 6 sts twice, pull tightly, and securely to WS.

Weave in all ends.

Thumb

Pick up and k 2 (4, 4, 4) sts just above and to the right of thumb opening and with the 10 (10, 10, 12) sts from holder divide onto three dpns—12 (14, 14, 16) sts. Work even to desired length to tip of thumb (approx 14–18 rnds).

Next rnd: K2tog to end of rnd—6 (7 ,7, 8) sts.

Break yarn, leaving a 12"/30.5cm tail. Thread tapestry needle and draw through rem sts twice, pull tightly, and secure to WS.

Second Mitten

Work as for First Mitten but reverse spiral top shaping dec rnd as foll:

Dec rnd: *Ssk, k6 (7, 8, 9) sts, pm; rep from * to end of rnd.

Next rnd: K even.

Next and subsequent dec rnds: *Ssk, k to marker, sm; rep from * to end of rnd.

Complete as for First Mitten thumb.

Finishing

Weave in all ends.

FENCELINE INTERCHANGEABLE COLOR CHART

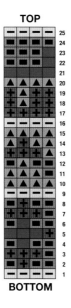

TOP

BOTTOM

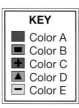

KEY

■	Color A
▣	Color B
✚	Color C
▲	Color D
⊟	Color E

Follow chart from bottom to top, right to left. Asterisks indicate thumb gusset increase rounds.

FOLK HEADBAND AND MITTENS

DESIGN BY SIGRID ARNOTT

The American fascination with immigrant folk art inspires many crafts—especially textiles. The felted and embroidered mittens of Scandinavia inspired this design, but the abstracted embroidery gives the headband and mitts an American simplicity. The headband uses an innovative technique to create its shape, resulting in a fast knit. The mittens and headband can be completed with an economical two skeins of yarn. ❧

HEADBAND

Size
One size

Finished Measurements
Before felting
Length: 19"/48.5cm
Width: 6½"/16.5cm
After felting
Length: Approx 17"/43cm
Width: 4½–5"/ 11.5–13cm

Materials
- Cascade 220 Heathers, 100% wool, 100g/3.5oz, 220yds/201m, Teal #4009, ¼ skein
- Appleton Crewel 2-ply, 100% wool in Lt. Green #354, Moss Green #404, Scarlet #504, and Dk. Pink #757, several yards each
- Size 8 (5mm) 24"/61cm circular needles or size to obtain gauge
- Size 6 (4mm) 24"/61cm circular needle
- Stitch markers
- Tapestry needle
- Chenille embroidery needle

Gauge
Before felting
20 sts and 23 rows = 4"/10 cm in St st with larger needles.
After felting
24½ sts and 35 rows = 4"/10 cm in St st.
Adjust needle size as necessary to obtain correct gauge.

MITTENS

Size
Children's Large (Woman's Medium)

Finished Measurements
Before felting
Circumference around palm: 9 (11)"/23 (28)cm
Length:10 (13½)"/25.5 (34)cm
After felting
Circumference around palm: 8 (10)"/20 (25)cm
Length: 7½ (10¼)"/19 (26)cm

Materials
- Cascade 220 Heathers, 100% wool, 100g/3.5oz, 220yds/201m, Teal #4009, 1 (2) skeins
- Appleton Crewel 2-ply, 100% wool, Lt. Green #354, Moss Green #404, Scarlet #504, and Dk. Green #757, several yards each
- Size 9 (5.5mm) double-pointed needles or size needed to obtain gauge
- Stitch markers
- Tapestry needle
- Chenille embroidery needle

Gauge
Before felting: 17½ sts and 20½ rows = 4"/10cm in St st.
After felting: 22 sts and 33 rows = 4"/10cm in St st.
Adjust needle size as necessary to obtain correct gauge.

PATTERN NOTE

Use a size 6 (4mm) circular needle, 24"/61cm long (although a 16"/40.5cm long needle would also work). As the size of the knitted piece decreases on the size 8 (5mm) needles, change to working with two 24"/61cm long circular needles (using one needle exclusively for each side). The "holding" needle hangs down out of the way, keeping its sts on the flexible cable. On the other "working" needle, slide the sts to the left needle tip and knit them onto the right needle tip. At the end of each half row (when all the sts for a side are on the right side of the needle), the sts are slid to the center of the cable. Now pick up the second needle, slide the sts to the left end, and begin knitting them with the right end of the same needle.

The headband is knitted with smaller needles and is lightly felted (or fulled) so that it is less stiff than the mittens and retains some elasticity. You can easily adjust the size by fulling more or using smaller needles for a smaller size.

HEADBAND INSTRUCTIONS

Using smaller needle, CO 156 sts; pm for beg of rnd and join, taking care not to twist sts.

Rnds 1–4: Work in k2 p2 rib for 4 rnds. Change to larger needle.

Rnd 5: K78, pm, k to end of rnd.

Rnd 6: *K to 2 sts before marker, ssk, k2, k2tog; rep from * around.

Rep Rnd 6 (dec by 4 sts each rnd) 13 more times—100 sts.

Last dec rnd: *K to marker and remove, k st before and next st tog using ssk, k2tog; rep from * once—96 sts.

Note: You will have created a long oval with a ribbed outer edge and a straight opening lengthwise down its center.

Close the center opening using a three-needle BO. With WS's tog, place 48 sts from each side next to each other and slide loops onto the left ends of their parallel needles. *Using a third needle (size is not important), slip it through a st on both the front and the back needles and k the 2 sts tog, rep from * until there are 2 sts on the right needle. BO the first st by slipping it over the second st*; rep from * to * to end of row. With 1 st rem on right needle, break yarn and pull it through the last st to secure. Weave in ends. (This will create a ridged center seam.)

Finishing

Felt by hand using alternately hot and cold soapy water until headband is desired size.

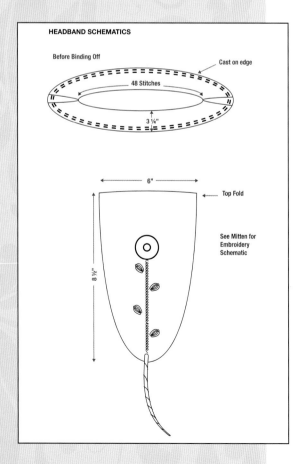

HEADBAND SCHEMATICS

Before Binding Off

Cast on edge

48 Stitches

3 ¼"

6"

Top Fold

See Mitten for Embroidery Schematic

8 ½"

Twisted Ties

Use a tapestry needle to thread a 1yd/1m length of yarn 1"/2.5cm through the center bottom of the headband. Using the headband to anchor the yarn over, twist the yarn by hand until it begins to twist back on itself. Pull the yarn through the fabric so that half of the length is on each side. Keeping the twist in the yarn, tie the two ends tog, then release so that the two ends twist tightly tog. Dampen the ties and felt them by rubbing them between your palms.

Embroidery

This project uses a few easy-to-perfect sts. Before starting to embroider your mittens, practice on a swatch.

Directions refer to the front, back, and inside of the fabric. The inside is precisely that: sandwiched in the thick felt, between the front and back, hidden from view.

All sts are done with the yarn doubled. To double, thread one end through the eye and pull the needle to the center.

Try not to use knots on the back of your knitting—it's uncomfortable. Instead try using a backstitch.

Backstitch

From the front put the threaded needle into the felted fabric about 1"/2.5cm from where you want to begin. Pass the needle inside the felted fabric and come up again to the front 1/8"/2–3mm past where you want to start (A in backstitch figure). Pull thread so that the tails just disappear into the fabric. Make a backstitch by putting the needle point down (from front to back) about 1/8"/2–3mm in front of this point (B) and then bringing the point up again at A. Now pull the needle and thread all the way through.

Finish in the same way. Make a tiny back stitch, then bury the yarn in the fabric. Cut the yarn close to the fabric, then stretch the fabric to swallow up the tails.

Running Stitch

Bring needle to front. Pass over front and down to back the desired length of st.

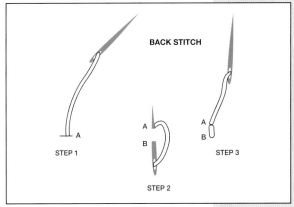

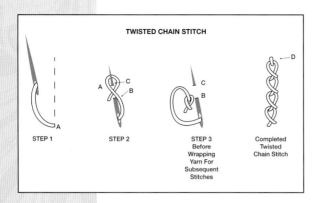

TWISTED CHAIN STITCH

STEP 1 STEP 2 STEP 3 Before Wrapping Yarn For Subsequent Stitches — Completed Twisted Chain Stitch

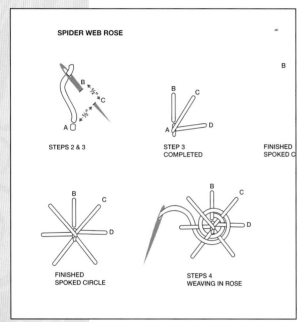

SPIDER WEB ROSE

STEPS 2 & 3 STEP 3 COMPLETED FINISHED SPOKED C

FINISHED SPOKED CIRCLE STEPS 4 WEAVING IN ROSE

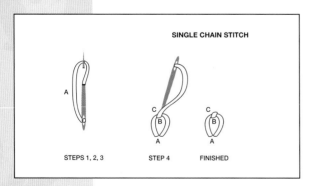

SINGLE CHAIN STITCH

STEPS 1, 2, 3 STEP 4 FINISHED

Twisted Chain Stitch

Step 1: Bring the needle and thread up on the front side in the center of the line you want to define at A.

Step 2: Put needle down ⅛"/2–3mm horizontally to the right at B, pass it to the back side of the fabric and bring the needle point up on the line about ¼"/4–5mm above at C. Leave the needle in the fabric and wrap the yarn in a loop underneath the needle from right to left. Pull the needle through the fabric and adjust the tension of the loop.

Rep step 2 for length of line.

Spiderweb Rose

First make a seven-spoked circle.

Step 1: Using about 1yd/1m Dk. Pink doubled, bring the threaded needle up and make a single backstitch A.

Step 2: Make a spoke above the st by bringing the tip of the needle down ½"/1.25cm above backstitch A.

Step 3: Bring the needle back up to the front ½"/1.25cm away on the circle's perimeter and ½"/1.25cm from the center.

Step 4: *Pass the needle under the center backstitch and then ½"/1.25cm back out to the circle's perimeter, putting the needle down into the fabric½"/1.25cm from where it came up.* Rep from * to * twice more to make seven spokes.

Step 5: Pull the needle and thread up in center of the wheel and weave thread under and over the spokes using the eye end of the needle. When the center is ½"/1.25cm across finish with Dk. Pink.

Step 6: Cont with Scarlet until the rose is 1"/2.5cm across and the spokes are completely covered.

Single Chain Stitch

Step 1: Bring the needle and yarn up at the front at the leaf's base (A) and then put the needle's point down in the exact same spot.

Step 2: Leaving the needle in the fabric, bring the tip up at the desired length of loop (B).

Step 3: Wrap the yarn under the needle, hold the loop with your thumb, and pull the needle and thread to the front.

Step 4: Put needle down on the other side of the loop (C) to make a small st to secure loop.

Refer to the photograph for st placement. Begin with the rose, placing it where shown or as desired. Sew the center ½"/1.25cm in Dk. Pink and finish with Scarlet.

Next sew the twisted chain stem starting at the bottom and finishing just under the rose using Moss Green. Sew the center leaf veins with simple running sts in Lt. Green. Each center vein is ½"/1.25cm long, starts about ⅛"/2–3mm from the twisted chain stem and slopes up at a 45-degree angle. The veins are made with simple running sts. Catch the yarn on the back between sts so that it will not loop on fingers. Finish by outlining the leaves with single chain sts in Moss Green that surround the running sts.

MITTEN INSTRUCTIONS

Cuff

Using dpns, CO 35 (48) sts; divide sts evenly on four dpns. Pm for beg of rnd and join, taking care not to twist sts.

Knit 4 rnds in St st.

Work 6 rnds in garter st (k 1 rnd, p 1 rnd).

Knit 10 (14) rnds in St st.

Thumb Gusset

Right Hand

Rnd 1: Remove marker, k2, pm, k2, pm, k to end of rnd.

Rnd 2: K to first marker, sm, inc 1 st using a backward loop, k to second marker, inc 1 st before it using a backward loop, sm, k to end of rnd.

Rnd 3: K, sm.

Rep Rnds 2 and 3 until there are 10 (14) sts between markers.

Left Hand

Rnd 1: Remove marker, k15 (18), pm. K2, pm, k to end of rnd. Complete as for right hand from Rnd 2 to end.

Main Mitten

Rnd 1: K first 2 sts of rnd, then sl sts between markers onto waste yarn. Pull slack out of yarn and tightly CO 2 sts using the backward loop method, then k to end of rnd—35 (48) sts.

K even in St st for 12 (14) rnds, about 2¼ (2¾)"/5.5 (7) cm above top of thumb gusset.

Decreases

For Women's Medium only:

Rnd 1: *K6, k2tog; rep from * around—42 sts.

Rnds 2–7: K 6 rnds even.

For Children's Large and Women's Medium:

Rnd 1: *K5, k2tog; rep from * around—30 (36) sts.

Rnds 2–5: K 4 rnds even.

Rnd 6: *K4, k2tog; rep from * around—25 (30) sts.

Rnds 7–9: K 3 rnds even.

Rnd 10: *K3, k2tog; rep from * around—20 (24) sts.

Rnds 11–12: K 2 rnds even.

Rnd 13: *K2, k2tog; rep from * around—15 (18) sts.

Rnd 14: K 1 rnd even.

Rnd 15: *K1, k2tog; rep from * around—10 (12) sts.

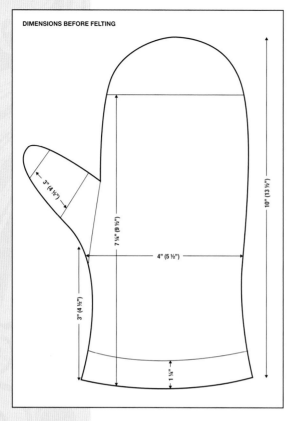

DIMENSIONS BEFORE FELTING

3" (4 ½")

7 ½" (9 ½")

4" (5 ½")

3" (4 ½")

1 ¼"

10" (13 ½")

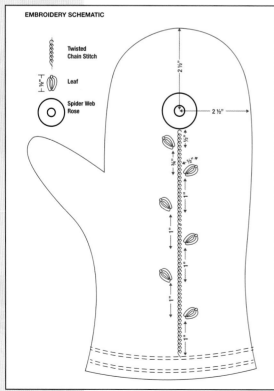

EMBROIDERY SCHEMATIC

Twisted Chain Stitch

Leaf

¼"

Spider Web Rose

2 ½"

2 ½"

¾"

½"

1"

1"

1"

1"

1"

Rnd 16: K2tog around—5 (6) sts.

Break yarn, leaving about 6"/15cm tail.

With tapestry needle, thread tail through rem loops, pull tight, and secure to WS.

Thumb

Transfer the 10 (14) sts from waste yarn to two needles. Using working yarn, pick up 1 st through side loop of a st next to thumb hole, pick up 2 sts in the CO sts, pick up another st through side loop of a st next to thumb hole—14 (18) sts.

K 9 (12) rnds in St st.

Decreases

Rnd 1: *K5 (7), k2tog, rep from * once—12 (16) sts.

Rnd 2: K 1 rnd.

Rnd 3: *K2, k2tog; rep from * around—9 (12) sts.

Rnd 4: *K1, k2tog; rep from * around—6 (8) sts.

Rnd 5: K2tog around—3 (4) sts.

Break yarn, leaving about 6"/15cm tail.

With tapestry needle, thread tail through rem loops, pull tight, and secure to WS.

Felting Mittens

Felt mittens by hand by vigorously washing and rubbing them together in alternating hot and cold soapy water until they are the desired size. In this way, you can closely watch the size and form the mittens to fit your hands. The mittens can also be felted in a washing machine by putting them in a lingerie bag with a pair of jeans (or something else that will provide friction but no lint) and a hot wash cycle. Keep resetting the length of the wash cycle until the mittens are the desired size. Try to remove them before the spin cycle, rinse in cold water, shape to your hand's shape, and air dry.

Hint: To test your felting technique, practice on the gauge swatch, remembering that it's a lot more work to felt the mittens than the swatch.

Embroidery

The mitten embroidery is the same as the headband. If desired, the stem can be shortened and the bottom leaves omitted.

PERUVIAN CH'ULLU HAT AND FINGERLESS GLOVES

DESIGN BY ELANOR LYNN

As a child, my primary visual reference for Andean culture was Herge's Tin Tin adventure *Prisoners of the Sun*. More recently, I've discovered the vast online textile collection of the Brooklyn Museum. These two *Ch'ullus* are inspired by an intricate contemporary example in this rich tradition.

The original includes shells on the earflaps, woven chin ties, and a tassel. The fingerless gloves are worked with a solid-color palm, with the upper portion knitted in this rich traditional Andean style. ❧

CH'ULLU

Size
Women's Medium

Finished Measurements
Circumference at head: 23"/58.5cm
Length: 14"/35.5cm (without ties)

Materials
- ◆ Cascade Pure Alpaca,100% Baby Alpaca, 100g/3.75oz, 220yds/200m, Red #3003 (A), Indigo #3025 (B), Ochre #3012 (C), White #3033 (D), Green #3019 (E), Magenta #3036 (F), Maroon #3047 (G), 1 skein each

- ◆ Sizes 1 (2.25mm), 2 (2.75mm), 3 (3.25mm), and 5 (3.75mm) straight needles

- ◆ Sizes 1 (2.25mm), 2 (2.75mm), and 3 (3.25mm) double-pointed and 16"/40.5cm long Circular needle

- ◆ Tapestry needle

Gauge
34 sts and 38 rows = 4"/10 cm in St st with size 5 (3.75mm) needles.
Adjust needle as necessary to obtain correct gauge.

FINGERLESS GLOVES

Size
Woman's Medium

Finished Measurements
Circumference at wrist: 6½"/16.5cm

Materials
- ◆ Cascade Pure Alpaca 100% Baby Alpaca, 100g/3.75oz, 220yds/200m, Red #3003 (A), Indigo #3025 (B), Ochre #3012 (C), White #3033 (D), Green #3019 (E), Magenta #3036 (F), Maroon #3047 (G), 1 skein each

- ◆ Sizes 1 (2.25mm), 2 (2.75mm), 3 (3.25mm), and 5 (3.75mm) straight needles

- ◆ Sizes 1 (2.25mm), 2 (2.75mm), and 3 (3.25mm) double-pointed and 16"/40.5cm long Circular needle

- ◆ Tapestry needle

Gauge
34 sts and 38 rows = 4"/10 cm in St st with size 5 (3.75) needle.
Adjust needle as necessary to obtain correct gauge.

PATTERN NOTES

The hat is worked in multicolor intarsia/stranded knitting. Due to the formidable number of ends to weave in for the seven-color version, you may wish to line your hat to avoid hours of finishing work. However, you then will lose the beauty of the stranding on the inside. Be sure to weave in the nonworking yarn when carried more than 4 sts. Also be sure to twist yarns at every color change. For the three-color version, since only two colors are used at one time, I've converted the pattern into round knitting. There is sufficient yardage to knit all three projects below.

When working charts maintain pattern multiples, continuing pattern on any extra stitches.

THREE-COLOR *CH'ULLU*

INSTRUCTIONS

With size 2 (2.75mm) dpns and A, CO 8 sts.

Pm at beg of rnd and join, taking care not to twist sts.

Rnd 1: Knit.

Rnd 2 and all even rnds through Rnd 22: Knit.

Rnd 3: Inc 1 st in each st–16 sts.

Rnd 5: Inc 1 st in each st–32 sts.

Rnd 7: Knit.

Rnd 9: (Inc 1 st in next st, k1) 16 times–48 sts.

Rnds 11, 13, 15: Knit.

Rnd 17: (Inc 1 st in next st, k2) 16 times–64 sts.

Rnd 19: (Inc 1 st in next st, k3) 16 times–80 sts.

Rnd 21: (Inc 1 st in next st, k7) 10 times—90 sts.

Change to size 3 (3.25mm) dpns or circular needle.

Rnds 23–26: With E and B, work Chart A, Rows 1–4.

Rnd 27: With B, inc 22 sts evenly across rnd—112 sts.

Rnd 28: With E, knit.

Rnds 29–43: With E and A, work Chart C, Rows 1–15 inc 8 sts evenly spaced within D sections on Rows 10, 12, and 14 of chart for a total of 24 sts inc'd—136 sts.

Rnd 44: With B, k1, inc 1 st in next 2 sts, k to last 3 sts, inc 1 st in next 2 sts, k1—140 sts.

Rnds 45–48: With B and A, work Chart A, Rnds 1–4.

Rnd 49: With A, inc 20 sts evenly across rnd—160 sts.

Rnds 50–94: Work Chart D with E and B.

Rnd 95: With E, k 1 rnd.

Rnds 96, 97, and 100: With size 1 (2.25mm) needle and B, knit.

Rnd 98: With B, k3, *with A, k3, with B, k3* end with A, k1.

Rnd 99: With A, k1, *with B, k3, with A, k3; rep from *, end with B, k3. Turn work so that you work the following rnd with WS facing.

Rnd 101 (WS): With size 5 (3.75mm) needles and B, BO 18 sts; with size 1 (2.25mm) needles k next 44; with size 5 (3.75mm) needles BO 35 sts; with size 1 (2.25mm) needles k next 44; with size 5 (3.75mm) needles BO rem sts.

Left Earflap

Row 1 (RS): Cont with size 3 (3.25mm) needles and B, k4; with E, k37; with B, k4—45 sts.

Row 2: With B, k4; with E and A, work Chart E, Row 1 over 37 sts; with B, k4.

Row 3: With B, k3, k2tog; with A and E, work Chart E, Row 2 over 35 sts; with B, k2tog, k3—43 sts.

Row 4: With B, k3, p2tog; with E and A, work Chart E, Row 3 over 33 sts; with B, ssp, k3—41 sts.

Cont as est, dec 2 sts every row until 9 sts rem.

Next row: Cont with B, k3, k3tog, k3—7 sts.

Next row (WS): Knit.

Next row: With E, k2; with B, k3; with E, k2.

Rep previous row, keeping nonworking yarn to the front of work.

Next row: With E, k3; with B, k1; with E, k3.

Rep previous row, keeping nonworking yarn to the front of work.

Next row: With E, k7.

K 63 rows.

Next row: K2, k3tog, k2—5 sts.

K 1 row.

Next row: K1, k3tog, k1—3 sts.

Next row: Knit.

Next row: K3tog.

Break yarn and draw through final loop.

Right Earflap

Rep as for Left Earflap.

Finishing

Sew short back seam to close BO edge. Close CO edge.

Weave in all ends.

SEVEN-COLOR *CH'ULLU*

INSTRUCTIONS

With size 3 (3.25mm) straight needles and A, CO 10 sts.

Row 1 (RS): Knit.

Row 2 and all even rows through Row 22: K1, purl to last st, k1.

Row 3: K1, (inc 1 st in next st) 8 times, k1—18 sts

Row 5: K1, (inc 1 st in next st) 16 times, k1—34 sts.

Row 7: Knit.

Row 9: K1, (inc 1 st in next st, k1) 16 times, k1—50 sts.

Rows 11, 13, and 15: Knit.

Row 17: K1 (inc 1 st in next st, k2) 16 times, k1—66 sts.

Row 19: K1 (inc 1 st in next st, k15) 4 times, k1—70 sts.

Rows 21–24: With B and C, work Chart A, Rows 1–4.

Row 25: With C, inc 18 sts evenly across row—88 sts.

Row 26: With D, inc 1 st in next st, p to last st, inc 1 st in next st—90 sts.

Rows 27–36: With D, E and A, work Chart B, Rows 1–10.

Row 37: With D, knit.

Rows 38–41: With A and E, work Chart A, Rows 1–4.

Row 42: With E, inc 24 sts evenly across row—114 sts.

Row 43: With D, knit.

Rows 44–58: With D, E, F, and G, work Chart C, Rows 1–15, inc 8 sts evenly spaced within D sections on Rows 9, 11, and 13 of chart—138 sts.

Row 59: With D, k1, inc 1 st in next 2 sts, k to last 3 sts, inc 1 st in next 2 sts, k1—142 sts.

Rows 60–63: With F and B, work Chart A, Rows 1–4.

Row 64: With B, inc 20 sts evenly across row—162 sts.

Rows 65–109: Work Chart D with all colors.

Row 110: With D, k 1 row.

Rows 111, 112, and 115: With size 1 (2.25mm) needles and B, knit.

Row 113: With B, k4, *with A, k3, with B, k3; rep from * to end.

Row 114: *With B, k3, with A, k3; rep from *, end with B, k4.

Row 116: With size 5 (3.75mm) needles and B, BO 18 sts; with size 1 (2.25mm) needles k next 44; with size 5 (3.75mm) needles, BO 35 sts; with size 1 (2.25mm) needles k next 44; with size 5 (3.75mm) needles, BO rem sts.

Left Earflap

Row 1 (RS): Cont with size 3 (3.25mm) needles, with B, k4; with D, k37; with B, k4—45 sts.

Row 2: With B, k4; with all colors except A and B, work Chart E, Row 1 over 37 sts; with B, k4.

Row 3: With B, k3, k2tog; with all colors except A and B, work Chart E, Row 2 over 35 sts; with B, k2tog, k3—43 sts.

Row 4: With B, k3, p2tog; with all colors except A and B, work Chart E, Row 3 over 33 sts; with B, ssp, k3—41 sts.

Cont as est, dec 2 sts every row until 9 sts rem.

Cont with B, k3, k3tog, k3—7 sts.

K 67 rows.

Next row: K2, k3tog, k2—5 sts.

K 1 row.

Next row: K1, k3tog, k1—3 sts.

K 1 row.

Next row: K3tog.

Break yarn and draw through final loop.

Right Earflap

Rep for Right Earflap.

Finishing

Sew mattress st seam. Close CO edge. Weave in all ends.

Optional: Line with fleece.

FINGERLESS GLOVE INSTRUCTIONS

With size 1 (2.25mm) needles and B, CO 58 sts.

Row 1 (RS): Knit.

Rows 2, 5, and 6: Knit.

Row 3: With B, k4, *with A, k3, with B, k3; rep from * to end.

Row 4: *With B, k3, with A, k3; rep from *, end with B, k4.

Rows 7–11: Change to size 3 (3.25mm) needles. With C and B, work Chart A, Rows 1–5.

Row 12: With D, knit.

(**Note:** Sl sts to other end of circular needles so that you will be working one RS row after another RS row. Subsequently, all even rows will be RS rows and all odd rows will be WS rows.)

Rows 13–22: With D, A, and E, work Chart B, Rows 1–10 (**Note:** On Row 13, dec 1 st 1 st from beg of row—57 sts.)

Rows 23–26: With C and B, work Chart A, Rows 1–4. (**Note:** On Row 23, inc 1 st 1 st from beg of row—58 sts.)

Row 27: With B, inc 14 sts evenly across row—72 sts.

Rows 28–43: With A, work in St st.

Row 44: K28, with size 5 (3.75mm) needle BO 15 sts, k28—57 sts.

Row 45: K1, p27, ssp, p26, k1—56 sts.

Rows 46–55: Work 10 rows even.

Row 56: Change to size 1 (2.25mm) needles. (K7, M1) 3 times, k14, (M1, k7) 3 times—62 sts.

Rows 57 and 59: K1, purl to last st, k1.

Row 58: (K7, M1, k1, M1) 3 times, k14, (M1, k1, M1, k7) 3 times—74 sts.

Row 60: With size 5 (3.75mm) needles, BO 44 sts.

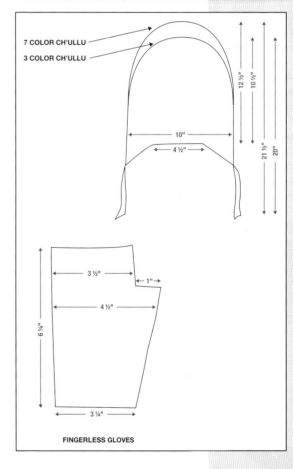

7 COLOR CH'ULLU

3 COLOR CH'ULLU

12 ½"

10 ½"

10"

4 ½"

21 ½"

20"

3 ½"

1"

4 ½"

6 ¼"

3 ¼"

FINGERLESS GLOVES

Join Finger Openings

With size 1 (2.25mm) needle, pick up 3 sts from the middle point of BO edge (9th, 19th, and 29th sts).

Returning to sts on Row 60, (work three-needle BO on next st, BO 9 sts) 3 times, BO rem sts.

Break yarn leaving 14"/35.5cm tail.

Finishing

Sew mattress st seam. Weave in all ends.

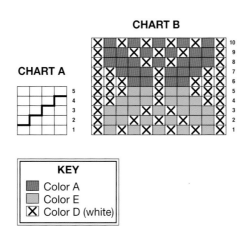

CHART B

CHART A

KEY

Color A
Color E
X Color D (white)

CHART C

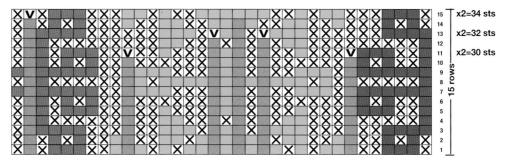

x2=34 sts
x2=32 sts
x2=30 sts
15 rows

Full Repeat=56 sts on row 1 &
68 sts on row 15

(Only half each of pink and maroon motifs are shown.)

KEY

Color A
Color E
Color
Color
X Color D (white)
V Color

CHART D

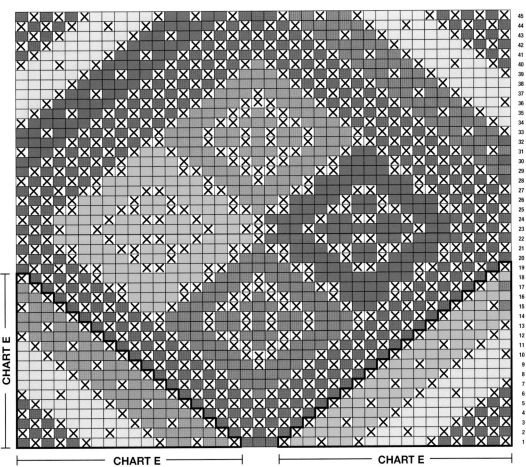

45
44
43
42
41
40
39
38
37
36
35
34
33
32
31
30
29
28
27
26
25
24
23
22
21
20
19
18
17
16
15
14
13
12
11
10
9
8
7
6
5
4
3
2
1

CHART E

├─────── CHART E ───────┤   ├─────── CHART E ───────┤

KEY	
	Color A
	Color B
	Color C
X	Color D
	Color E
	Color F
	Color G

KNITTING ABBREVIATIONS

beg	begin(s), beginning	psso	pass slip st(s) over
BO	bind off	pwise	purlwise (as if to purl)
CC	contrast color	rem	remain(s), remaining
cm	centimeter(s)	rep(s)	repeat(s), repeated, repeating
CO	cast on	rnd(s)	round(s)
cont	continue, continuing	RH	right-hand
dec(s)	decrease, decreasing, decreases	RS	right side (of work)
dpn	double-pointed needle(s)	revsc	reverse single crochet (crab st)
est	establish, established	sc	single crochet
foll	follow(s), following	sl	slip, slipped, slipping
inc(s)	increase(s), increasing	ssk	[slip 1 st knitwise] twice from left needle to right needle, insert left needle tip into fronts of both slipped sts, knit both sts together from this position (decrease)
k	knit		
k1f&b	knit into front then back of same st (increase)		
k1f,b,&f	knitting into front, back, then front again of same st (increase 2 sts)	ssp	[slip 1 st knitwise] twice from left needle to right needle, return both sts to left needle and purl both together through back loops
k1-tbl	knit 1 st through back loop		
k2tog	knit 2 sts together (decrease)	st(s)	stitch(es)
k2tog-tbl	knit 2 sts together through back loops	St st	stockinette stitch
kwise	knitwise (as if to knit)	tbl	through back loop
LH	left-hand	tog	together
m(s)	marker(s)	w&t	wrap next stitch, then turn work (often used in short rows)
MC	main color		
mm	millimeter(s)	WS	wrong side (of work)
M1	make 1 (increase)	wyib	with yarn in back
M1k	make 1 knitwise	wyif	with yarn in front
M1p	make 1 purlwise	yb	yarn back
pat(s)	pattern(s)	yf	yarn forward
p	purl	yo	yarn over
p1f&b	purl into front then back of same st (increase)	*	repeat instructions from *
p1-tbl	purl 1 st through back loop	( )	alternate measurements and/or instructions
p2tog	purl 2 sts together (decrease)	[ ]	instructions to be worked as a group a specified number of times
pm	place marker		

YARN RESOURCES

Alpaca with a Twist
www.alpacawithatwist.com

Berroco
www.berroco.com

Black Water Abbey Yarns
www.abbeyyarns.com

Brown Sheep
www.brownsheep.com

Cascade Yarns
www.cascadeyarns.com

Classic Elite
www.classiceliteyarns.com

Drops
www.garnstudio.com

Frog Tree
www.frogtreeyarns.com

HelmiVuorelmaOy, Finland
kauppa.vuorelma.net

ístex
www.istex.is

Kerry Woolen Mills
www.kerrywoollenmills.ie

Lion Brand Yarns
www.lionbrand.com

Louet
www.louet.com

Red Fish Dyeworks
www.redfishdyeworks.com

Reynolds Yarns
www.jcacrafts.com

Rowan
www.rowanyarns.co.uk

Sublime Yarns
www.sublimeyarns.com

Stitch Diva Studios
www.stitchdiva.com

Tilli Tomas
www.tillitomas.com

STANDARD YARN WEIGHT SYSTEM

Categories of yarn, gauge ranges, and recommended needle and hook sizes

Yarn Weight Symbol & Category Names	0 Lace	1 Super Fine	2 Fine	3 Light	4 Medium	5 Bulky	6 Super Bulky
Type of Yarns in Category	Fingering 10 count crochet thread	Sock, Fingering, Baby	Sport, Baby	DK, Light Worsted	Worsted, Afghan, Aran	Chunky, Craft, Rug	Bulky, Roving
Knit Gauge Range* in Stockinette Stitch to 4 inches	33–40** sts	27–32 sts	23–26 sts	21–24 sts	16–20 sts	12–15 sts	6–11 sts
Recommended Needle in Metric Size Range	1.5–2.25 mm	2.25–3.25 mm	3.25–3.75 mm	3.75–4.5 mm	4.5–5.5 mm	5.5–8 mm	8mm and larger
Recommended Needle U.S. Size Range	000 to 1	1 to 3	3 to 5	5 to 7	7 to 9	9 to 11	11 and larger
Crochet Gauge* Ranges in Single Crochet to 4 inch	32–42 double crochets**	21–31 sts	16–20 sts	12–17 sts	11–14 sts	8–11 sts	5–9 sts
Recommended Hook in Metric Size Range	Steel*** 1.6–1.4mm Regular hook 2.25mm	2.25–3.5 mm	3.5–4.5 mm	4.5–5.5 mm	5.5–6.5 mm	6.5–9 mm	9mm and larger
Recommended Hook U.S. Size Range	Steel*** 6, 7, 8 Regular hook B–1	B–1 to E–4	E–4 to 7	7 to I–9	I–9 to K–10 ½	K–10 ½ to M–13	M–13 and larger

* GUIDELINES ONLY: The above reflect the most commonly used gauges and needle or hook sizes for specific yarn categories.

** Lace weight yarns are usually knitted or crocheted on larger needles and hooks to create lacy, openwork patterns. Accordingly, a gauge range is difficult to determine. Always follow the gauge stated in your pattern.

*** Steel crochet hooks are sized differently from regular hooks—the higher the number, the smaller the hook, which is reverse of regular hook sizing.

This Standards & Guidelines booklet and downloadable symbol artwork are available at: YarnStandards.com.

ABOUT THE DESIGNERS

Sigrid Arnott is a Minneapolis writer, designer, seamstress, and boy rancher. She writes about her analog exploits at www.analogme.typepad.com.

Dawn Brocco began her designing career working freelance for most of the major knitting publications. She has been self-publishing for the past thirteen years and now has more than one hundred patterns available. Her style embraces classic design with modern twists and whimsical design based on a love of nature. You can find Dawn Brocco Knitwear Designs at www.dawnbrocco.com and you can reach Dawn at dawn@dawnbrocco.com.

Elinor Brown lives with her husband, two kids, and two dogs in Columbus, Ohio, where she attends medical school at Ohio State University. Her knitting designs have appeared in *Interweave Knits, Knitscene, PopKnits, Twist Collective, Vogue Knitting*, and *Yarn Forward*. All can be found on Ravelry (www.ravelry.com/designers/elinor-brown), or on her blog, Exercise before Knitting (exercisebeforeknitting.com).

Beth Brown-Reinsel has been teaching knitting workshops nationally, as well as internationally, for more than twenty years. She wrote the book *Knitting Ganseys* and has recently filmed the DVD *Knitting Ganseys with Beth Brown-Reinsel*. Her articles have appeared in *Threads; Cast On; Interweave Knits; Shuttle, Spindle, Dye Pot; Vogue Knitting*; and *Knitters* magazines. She continues to design for her own pattern line, available at www.knittingtraditions.com. Beth lives happily in Vermont.

Lily M. Chin is a knitter and crocheter who has worked in the yarn industry for over twenty-five years as a designer, instructor, and author of books on knitting and crochet. She has created couture crochet for the New York Fashion Week runway collections of designers Ralph Lauren, Vera Wang, Diane von Furstenberg, and Isaac Mizrahi. Learn more at www.lilychinsignaturecollection.com.

Donna Druchunas is the author of numerous books, including *Successful Lace Knitting: Celebrating the Work of Dorothy Reade, Ethnic Knitting Exploration: Lithuania, Iceland, and Ireland*, and *Arctic Lace: Knitted Projects and Stories Inspired by Alaska's Native Knitters*. She spent four months this year traveling in Europe teaching knitting workshops and doing research for her next book, which will be about knitting in Lithuania. Visit her website at www.sheeptoshawl.com.

Anne Caroll Gilmour owned and operated Wildwest Woolies, a full-spectrum textile arts shop in Evanston, Wyoming, for nearly six years. She now lives in the beautiful Wasatch Mountains near Park City, Utah, where she works in her studio and also teaches workshops in spinning, weaving, and knitting. Her work has been featured in various textile publications and many galleries, museums, and private collections worldwide. Many of her knitwear patterns are available on her website: www.wildwestwoolies.com

Jennifer Hansen is the founder and chief designer of Stitch Diva Studios. She lives in Los Gatos, California, where she is a full-time crochet and knit designer, teacher, and writer. Her innovative crochet work has been featured in various books, magazines, and television shows, including *Vogue Knitting, Interweave Crochet, The Happy Hooker, The Encyclopedia of Crochet*, and *Knitty Gritty*.

Janel Laidman has been obsessed with knitting since 1980, when she discovered that Danish girls could knit socks and learn physics at the same time. In the quest to reach the same lofty heights of coolness, she taught herself to knit too. Today Janel spends her time designing socks and other knitted garments, writing knitting books, feeding tulips to the deer, and knitting, of course! Janel is the author of *The Enchanted Sole: Legendary Socks for Adventurous Knitters*.

Elanor Lynn relocated from Brooklyn, New York, to Hollywood, California, three years ago. Since then, she's been knitting lots of palm trees into tapestries. She's currently exploring "handwritten" fonts in text-based work.

Hélène Magnússon is best known for her research around the traditional Icelandic intarsia that was seen in knitted inserts in shoes in Iceland in the past centuries. Her book, *Icelandic Knitting: Using Rose Patterns*, is available in three languages. She is a French native but a true Icelandic knitter, and has an Icelandic family. Find out more about her on her website: www.helenemagnusson.com.

Heather Ordover's latest joy has been writing and editing the first pattern book in the series *What Would Madame Defarge Knit? Creations Inspired by Classic Characters*. Prior to that, she spent her time writing and recording essays for *Cast-On: A Podcast for Knitters* and currently hosts her own long-running podcast, *CraftLit: A Podcast for Crafters Who Love Books* (think "audiobook with benefits"). Her crafty writing has appeared in *Spin-Off, WeaveZine*, and *The Arizona Daily Star*.

Lizbeth Upitis is author of *Latvian Mittens*, published by Schoolhouse Press. She is a knitting designer, author, and editor of articles and books for *Knitters* magazine, *Interweave Press, Vogue Knitting*, Schoolhouse Press, and XRX Books.

First published in 2012 by Voyageur Press, an imprint of MBI Publishing Company, 400 First Avenue North, Suite 300, Minneapolis, MN 55401 USA

Voyageur Press titles are also available at discounts in bulk quantity for industrial or sales-promotional use. For details write to Special Sales Manager at MBI Publishing Company, 400 First Avenue North, Suite 300, Minneapolis, MN 55401 USA.

To find out more about our books, visit us online at www.voyageurpress.com.

Editor: Kari Cornell
Design Manager: James Kegley
Designer: Erin Fahringer
Photography: Sue Flander and Janine Kosel
Model Photography: rau+barber
Model Stylist: Libby Fransen
Hair and makeup: Angelia

ISBN-13: 978-0-7603-4065-3

Printed in China

Library of Congress Cataloging-in-Publication Data

Knitting hats & mittens from around the world: heirloom patterns in a variety of styles and techniques / Kari Cornell, Editor;
photographs by Sue Flanders and Janine Kosel.
     p. cm.
ISBN 978-0-7603-4065-3 (hbk.)
1. Knitting--Patterns. 2. Hats. 3. Mittens. I. Cornell, Kari A.
TT825.K6452 2012
746.43'2--dc23
                    2011048664

Photo Credits
Page 7: A Lapp family in Norway, wearing traditional handknit hats, c.1890. *Library of Congress Prints and Photographs Division, Landscape and marine views of Norway #LC-DIG-ppmsc-06257*
Page 45: Knitting girl, painted by William Adolphe Bourguereau, 1869. *Voyageur Press Archives*
Page 97: Vintage postcard, *Voyageur Press Archives*
Page 117: Navajo woman, holding yarn, c. 1904. 120925, *Library of Congress, Prints and Photographs Division, #LC-USZ62-120925*

ACKNOWLEDGMENTS

This fun and intriguing collection of hat and mitten sets came together with the help of several creative designers. Many thanks to all who contributed their talents to this book: Sigrid Arnott, Dawn Brocco, Elinor Brown, Beth Brown-Reinsel, Lily Chin, Donna Druchunas, Candace Eisner Strick, Anne Caroll Gilmour, Jennifer Hansen, Janel Laidman, Elanor Lynn, Hélène Magnússon, Heather Ordover, Kristin Spurkland, and Lizbeth Upitis. Collaborating with this great community of knitters is what makes my work fun, and I'm pleased to have the opportunity to be part of this creative process. I'm grateful to Donna Druchunas for digging into the history of knitting hats and mittens to write a thoughtful, fitting introduction to the book. Many, many thanks to Sue Flanders and Janine Kosel for the hours they dedicated to capturing just the right images for each of the projects. Thanks to the following locations for inviting Sue and Janine to use their settings as backdrops for the photos in this book: Kate Martinson, for use of her fantastic home and props; Gammelgarden in Scandia, MN; Fairhaven Farms in Fairhaven, MN; and Pioneer Park in Annandale, MN.

Special thanks to Rita Greenfeder for her technical editing expertise. A big thank-you to rau+barber for the top-notch photography, to stylist Libby Fransen for her keen eye for detail, and to hair and makeup artist Angelia for making the models look great. Thanks to Becky Pagel, James Kegley, and the rest of the design team for all that they do to make Voyageur Press books look their best. And, last but not least, many thanks to the American Swedish Institute in Minneapolis, for allowing us to take photos in their beautiful mansion.

INDEX